Robert Browning

HIS LIFE AND WORK

F. E. HALLIDAY

Robert Browning

HIS LIFE AND WORK

JUPITER BOOKS

© 1975 F. E. Halliday

First published in 1975 by Jupiter Books (London) Ltd
167 Hermitage Road, Harringay, London N.4

SBN 904041 360

Set in Monotype Plantin by The Lancashire Typesetting
Company, Limited, Bolton

Printed and bound in Great Britain by R. J. Acford Limited,
Chichester, Sussex

For JUNE OPIE

Contents

Acknowledgements

I AM grateful to all those who have supplied me with illustrations for this book, particularly Mr E. V. Quinn, Librarian of Balliol College, Oxford, Dr J. W. Herring, Director, and Mrs B. A. Coley, Librarian, of the Armstrong Browning Library, Baylor University, Texas, and Mr A. P. Buxton, Assistant Keeper of the Victoria and Albert Museum Library, all of whom have gone to considerable trouble on my behalf.

And I take this opportunity of thanking those who have helped me in other ways: the Librarians and staffs of the Cornwall County Library, the Morrab Library, Penzance, the St Ives Library, and the Deputy Keeper of the British Collection in the Tate Gallery.

Finally, once again I am indebted, and correspondingly grateful, to Sir John Summerson and Mr George Wingfield Digby, who have given me much valuable information about illustrations.

Preface

WHEN, as a small boy, I went away to boarding-school, I was given a red-backed book with the title: '*Macbeth:* A. W. Verity.' I felt sure that the play was written by somebody called Shakespeare, and it took me some time to discover that Mr Verity was merely what was called an editor, one who explained the decent obscurities of the poet and ignored the indecent ones. That was in 1916, and not long afterwards my form-master gave us, his pupils, the four lines of 'Parting at Morning' to paraphrase and explain. I was enchanted by the poem, and as my form-master was also my housemaster, a lover of Browning, and the man who was to become my first great friend, I too became a lover of Browning, and before I left school had read and re-read most of the shorter poems and some of the longer ones, such as *Pippa Passes*. For many boys, perhaps most, Shakespeare is their introduction to poetry, as distinct from verse, and there can be few whose introduction was Shakespeare and Browning. Yet so it was for me, and this explains why, when I was reading English at Cambridge, I shocked my supervisor by maintaining that Browning was a greater poet than Tennyson.

Perhaps I should have said 'more important' rather than 'greater', which simply indicated a personal preference. Although Browning was an accomplished musician he was not, at least in his long, his over-long poems, like Tennyson greatly concerned with the music of his lines, or in trimming and polishing phrases until the sound of the words themselves resembled the moan of doves or murmuring of bees, and it is significant that for me Tennyson's most memorable poems are dramatic monologues such as 'Ulysses' and 'Tiresias'. For it was Browning's dramatic monologues that so fascinated me: not the elegant simplicities of mythical characters, but the complex thoughts of real men and women like Shakespeare's and Chaucer's.

Of course Browning had his faults, more obvious faults than most great poets. Impatient, impetuous, he often wrote so quickly that he blurred his meaning, either by carelessness or by the leap of unconsciously associated ideas, which, as he told Ruskin, he expected his readers to follow; and sometimes he wrote so much that he became a garrulous bore. This was largely because of his belief that a poet must teach, and I for one have never had much sympathy with his teaching. Fortunately, however, he often forgot his mission, wrote carefully and briefly, and produced such masterpieces as the early 'My Last Duchess' and the late 'Imperante Augusto Natus Est – ', and above all the *Men and Women* of his middle period.

For there are three Robert Brownings, or at least two-and-a-half: first, the over-confident, ambitious, prolific, unsuccessful author of *Sordello*, last, his even more prolific successful successor, and between the two the devoted husband of Elizabeth Barrett, author of fifty poems about men and women, and shortly after her death of *Dramatis Personae* and *The Ring and the Book*.

But Browning is not only one of the greatest of English poets, he is also one of the most important, a revolutionary who broke away from conventional subjects and their conventional treatment, from myth, ode, sonnet and poetic diction, to write about real men and women in a language not far removed from real speech. He is, in brief, the founder of modern English poetry. Although Hardy detested what he called his bourgeois philosophy, and maintained – the very reverse of Browning – that the business of the poet is to reveal his own heart, without Browning he would not have written as he did about the all-important details of everyday life: old furniture, a second-hand suit. And without Browning the dramatic monologue of 'Prufrock' might well have been a very different poem. It appeared in 1917, when my German master assured me that its author, one T. S. Eliot, deserved to be spat upon from a very great height:

> Shall I say, I have gone at dusk through narrow streets
> And watched the smoke that rises from the pipes
> Of lonely men in shirt-sleeves, leaning out of windows ? –
>
> I should have been a pair of ragged claws
> Scuttling across the floors of silent seas.

There again is the illogical leap of unconsciously associated ideas, introduced by prosaic and apparently unimportant detail.

This book, however, is little concerned with the detail of scholarly research, but is a tribute to a poet who has given me a lifetime's pleasure, and an attempt to make him easier of access to others by quite simply relating his work to his life and the age in which he lived. As John Heminge and Henry Condell wrote of a greater poet than Browning: 'Reade him, therefore; and againe, and againe: And if then you do not like him, surely you are in some manifest danger, not to understand him.' Browning himself was in danger: 'Do you believe people understand *Hamlet* ?' he wrote, and as applied to his own work the last few words must not be taken too seriously. Rather, read the poems that are easy, or comparatively easy, to understand, and read also the letters of Browning and Elizabeth Barrett, for they are in the nature of a Browning poem, and therefore among the masterpieces of the English language.

St Ives
Cornwall
July 1974

I. LONDON 1812–1846

1. Early Years

1812–33

WHEN Robert Browning was born on 7 May 1812 Britain's twenty-year war with France was approaching its climax. A few weeks later, Wellington, advancing from his base in Portugal, defeated the French at Salamanca, occupied Madrid, and drove out Napoleon's brother Joseph, so-called King of Spain. But Napoleon himself had already crossed the Russian frontier, and was marching on Moscow at the head of an army of more than half a million men. And it was Napoleon's commercial tactics that had driven the United States and Britain into a short and futile war a week before this momentous invasion of Russia had begun.

At home, the mind of the old king George III had finally broken down after the death of his favourite daughter, and his eldest son George, a fifty-year-old rake, had become Prince Regent, the 'Prinny' of his boon companions. Then, four days after Browning's birth, the Prime Minister, Spencer Perceval, was shot dead in the lobby of the House of Commons by a crazy assassin with a grievance. There were plenty of others with grievances. The distresses caused by the war, high prices and economic change led to riots; the reactionary Tory government replied by adding 'frame-breaking' to its long list of capital offences, and in 1812 sixteen of these breakers of new-fangled wooden machines were executed.

Napoleon's occupation of Moscow was followed by fire and his compulsory, disastrous retreat through the snows and frosts of the late autumn of 1812; by his defeat at Leipzig in the following year, his abdication and exile to Elba, his escape, the Hundred Days and final defeat at Waterloo on 18 June 1815, a date that Browning, who forgot nothing, always professed he could not remember. Yet he was only three years old at the time. Britain, exhausted, impoverished, yet immensely enriched by the acquisition of a new Empire, emerged from the long struggle the greatest power in the world. So powerful not only because of its territorial expansion, but also because it led the way in the Industrial Revolution.

17

Even before the beginning of the war in 1793 there had been many inventions, particularly in the textile industry, that had begun the transformation of the old domestic system, that of spinning and weaving in the home, into a system of machines assembled in factories driven by water power, but now James Watt's invention of a steam engine that would turn a wheel led to the concentration of industry in factories on the coalfields of the north. The independent worker had become a wage-earner, forbidden to combine with others to better his condition, and at the mercy of his employer. Robert Browning may be said to have come in with the age of steam, factory, railway and gas – in 1813 Waterloo Bridge, only a few miles from his home, was lighted by gas. It was an exciting, though for some people unhappy, age in which to be born, a period of distress and savage repression by a government frightened by memories of the French Revolution, a repression that lasted until the victory of the Whigs in 1830 and passing of the Reform Bill after two years of struggle.

Robert Browning was not the only child of genius to be born at the beginning of the Regency decade. Charles Dickens was exactly three months older, Thackeray a few months older still, and Tennyson and Darwin were children of 1809. Elizabeth Barrett, destined to become Elizabeth Barrett Browning, was a girl of six when her future husband was born. There had been a comparable genesis of genius in the 1770s with the appearance of the leaders of the Romantic Movement: Wordsworth, Coleridge, Southey, Scott and Landor were all men of about forty in 1812, as were the painters Constable and Turner. Twenty years later came the second generation of Romantic poets: in 1812 Byron published the first two cantos of *Childe Harold*, the twenty-year-old Shelley had just been sent down from Oxford for his pamphlet on *The Necessity of Atheism*, and the seventeen-year-old Keats was a surgeon's apprentice on the northern outskirts of London. Carlyle, the same age as Keats, was training for the ministry at Edinburgh University.

The Brownings were originally a Dorset family, but in 1769, at the age of twenty, the poet's grandfather, another Robert, for that was the name of all the eldest sons, went to London to seek his fortune. An energetic, ambitious philistine, he became a senior clerk in the Bank of England and married a girl who had been born in the West Indies where she had inherited property. She died young, and their son Robert, born in 1782, was only seven at the time of her death, soon after which his father married again and had a large family by this second wife. Brought up by a jealous stepmother and a father who despised his literary and artistic bent, the boyhood of Robert ii, the poet's father, was an unhappy one. Then, instead of going to a university as he wished, at the age of twenty he was sent to the West Indian island of St Kitts to help to manage his mother's sugar plantation. That was in 1802, long before the abolition of slavery, a system he so detested that he returned to England as soon as he could. So furious was his father that he made him repay all the money he had spent on bringing him up, and ten years later, when the young man was engaged to Sarah Anna Wiedemann, he told her uncle that his niece 'would be thrown away on a man so evidently born to be hanged'. Driven to earn a living as best he could, Robert ii also became a clerk in the Bank of England, and in 1811 married Miss Wiedemann whom he took to live in a small house, Hanover Cottage, in Camberwell. It was there in the following year that the poet Robert Browning was born, followed two years later by his sister Sarianna, a name that was a contraction of his mother's, Sarah Anna.

Camberwell was an ideal home for the children. In spite of the rapidly growing population, recently foretold by Malthus in his famous essay, it was still little more than a village set in a pleasant wooded and rolling countryside, yet with the Thames, Westminster and City of London only two or three miles to the north. Then, across the fields to the south was the village of Dulwich where, at the time of Browning's birth, Sir John Soane – architect of the new Bank of England – was completing an art gallery to house a collection of pictures, the nucleus of which was those left by the Elizabethan actor Edward Alleyn, founder of Dulwich College.

As Browning was to write to Elizabeth Barrett some 25 years later:

that gallery I so love and so am grateful to – having been used to go there when a child, far under the age allowed by the regulations – those two Guidos, the wonderful Rembrandt of Jacob's vision, such a Watteau, the triumphant three Murillo pictures, a Giorgione music-lesson group, all the Poussins. . . . I have sate before one, some *one* of those pictures I had pre-determined to see, a good hour and then gone away . . . it used to be a green half-hour's walk over the fields.

He might have mentioned the pictures of Lairesse and his *Art of Painting*, a book which, as a boy, he read more often than any other in his father's library. However, he was to celebrate his work 25 years after Elizabeth's death.

A small house in a large garden in a village surrounded by fields, hedges and woods, the country's capital and an art gallery within easy walking distance, and in August the gaiety of a fair on the village green, where gipsies arrived to share in the fun. And inside the house there were books, six thousand of them.

For the boy's father was a devoted reader and collector of rare books, particularly by obscure or little-known authors. A bank clerk instead of the professor of classics that he might have become had he not been foiled by his father, he was nevertheless a good classical scholar with an unusual knowledge of French, Italian and Spanish literature as well. Fond of pictures, particularly the genre paintings of the Dutch school and English Hogarth, he was himself an artist in a modest way, with a gift for drawing rapid sketches of people from memory, and scenes such as those he had witnessed of slavery in St Kitts. Yet he was no bookworm, was something of an athlete, and lived to be nearly eighty-five without a day's illness in his life. Shortly before his own death, Browning was to describe this quiet, kindly, unassuming, unambitious man, the very antithesis of his grandfather and in some ways of himself, and the manner in which he encouraged his education:

> My Father was a scholar and knew Greek.
> When I was five years old, I asked him once
> 'What do you read about ?' 'The siege of Troy.'
> 'What is a siege and what is Troy ?' Whereat
> He piled up chairs and tables for a town,
> Set me a-top for Priam, called our cat. . . .[1]

Their cat played Helen, their dogs Agamemnon and Menelaus, while Paris skulked invisible under the footstool, and young Robert's prancing pony Achilles chased the fleeing page-boy Hector. Two or three years later his father gave him Pope's translation of the *Iliad* to read, and by the age of twelve 'the all-accomplished scholar' was thumbing his way through the original Greek.

His father was concerned mainly with the boy's intellectual development, and it was his mother who had the greater influence on his deeper emotional life. The daughter of a Scottish girl and a Hamburg shipping agent living in Dundee, she met her future husband when she and her sister Christiana were staying with an uncle in Camberwell. Christiana also met her future husband there, a local brewer called Silverthorne, so that her sons and their cousin Robert grew up together as neighbours and friends. No portrait of Robert's mother has survived, but according to another Camberwell friend, Alfred Domett, she had 'the *squarest* head and forehead I almost ever saw in a human being, putting me in mind, absurdly enough, no doubt, a of tea-chest or tea caddy.'[2] That was probably her father's German legacy, but for Scottish Carlyle she was 'the true type of a Scottish gentlewoman'. More revealing was John Kenyon's opinion that she was one of those who have no need to go to heaven, for they make it wherever they are. Browning used to say that he could not sit beside her without putting his hand round her waist, and how strong was the bond between them is revealed in a letter that he wrote to Elizabeth Barrett when he was thirty-four:

My mother continues indisposed. The connection between our ailings is no fanciful one. A few weeks ago when my medical adviser was speaking about the pain and its cause .. my mother sitting by me .. he exclaimed 'Why has anybody to search for a cause of whatever nervous disorder you may suffer from, when *there* sits your mother .. whom you absolutely resemble .. I can trace every feature &c. &c.'[3]

Unlike his father, his mother was essentially practical, and the household was mainly dependent on her management. She loved music, however, and would play the piano after her little son had gone to bed, where he would lie and listen, and one evening, when she had stopped, he ran down in tears to beg her to go on playing. She also loved nature, particularly flowers and small animals, and with them she would bribe him to take his medicine, one of his early memories being of her parasol hovering over a strawberry-bed while she looked for a speckled frog. It followed that, as a small boy, he himself began to collect and keep birds and animals, characteristically, unusual ones: owls and magpies, hedgehogs and monkeys, even an eagle and two snakes, which he and his mother cared for.

Music and animals – and religion. For his mother was deeply religious, though not, of course, a member of the Church of England, but a Scottish Dissenter, and it was to a Congregational Chapel in Walworth, about a mile north of Camberwell, that she took her two children, and her at first reluctant husband. 'My father and mother,' Browning wrote in 1845, 'went this morning to the very Independent Chapel where they took me all those years back, to be baptised – and where they heard, this morning, a sermon preached by the very minister who officiated on that other occasion!' Evidently he had not accompanied his parents, for though his mother's influence made the child 'passionately religious', he was to become even more independent than the Independents, and in *Christmas-Eve* to draw a not altogether flattering picture of a service in a Dissenting Chapel, which must have been based on old memories, though not of a prim, middle-class Walworth-Camberwell congregation:

> Nay, had but a single face of my neighbours
> Appeared to suspect that the preacher's labours
> Were help that the world could be saved without,
> 'Tis odds but I might have borne in quiet
> A qualm or two of my spiritual diet,

> Or (who can tell ?) perchance even mustered
>   Somewhat to urge in behalf of the sermon:
> But the flock sat on, divinely flustered,
>   Sniffing, methought, its dew of Hermon
> With such content in every snuffle,
> As the devil inside us loves to ruffle.
> My old fat woman purred with pleasure,
>   And thumb round thumb went twirling faster,
> While she, to his periods keeping measure,
>   Maternally devoured the pastor. . . .

But he was nearly forty when he wrote that, and little Robert Browning (like little Thomas Hardy), liked to dress up as a minister and, standing on a chair, preach to his young sister, until the terrified Sarianna began to cry, whereupon he would turn to an imaginary assistant and call, 'Pew-opener, remove that child.' An entry that he made in his diary at about the age of seven, 'Married two wives this morning,' was no doubt less orthodox than his preaching, and appears to have referred to two girls whom he had seen in chapel that morning.

He was a turbulent child, and to give his mother a little rest during the day he was sent to a nursery school kept by a neighbouring lady. So precocious was he, however, that other mothers began to complain that she was neglecting their children for the sake of 'bringing on Master Browning'. She replied that all boys had not got Master Browning's intelligence, but had to hint to his mother that it would be better for her school if he were withdrawn. There followed a period of home education: of painting in currant juice, for ordinary paint was poisonous to brush-suckers, of reading – and of writing. As he was to tell Elizabeth Barrett,

The first *composition* I ever was guilty of was something in *imitation* of Ossian, whom I had not read, but *conceived*, through two or three scraps in other books – I never can recollect *not* writing rhymes, but I knew they were nonsense even then; *this*, however, I thought exceedingly well of, and laid up for posterity under the cushion of a great arm-chair . . . I could not have been five years old.

There was no compulsory education in those days, but after an interval he was sent as a weekly-boarder to a preparatory school kept by two Misses Ready. Never before had he been away from home by himself, and at first was so unhappy that he chose as his tomb an old cistern on which a face was embossed, and beside it would sit chanting, 'In memory of unhappy Browning.' He soon recovered his spirits, however, and was to remember the devout Misses Ready by their singing of hymns by nonconformist Watts as ferociously they combed his hair:

> Lord, 'tis a pleasant thing to stand
> In gardens planted by Thy hand . . .
> Fools never raise their thoughts so high,
> Like *brutes* they live, like BRUTES they die.

Eventually he passed into the senior school of the Rev. Thomas Ready himself, but again was too intelligent to learn much, and preferred acting and producing plays of his own composition. His real education was at home during weekends and holidays, when he would ransack his father's library and read such out-of-the-way seventeenth-century books as the *Emblems* of Francis Quarles, and *Wonders of the Little World* by Nathaniel Wanley, a nonconformist minister who told horrific stories of strange births, lives, sufferings and deaths: odd but fascinating reading for an imaginative boy, and the source-book of a number of his poems, as the fifty volumes of the *Biographie Universelle* were to be of others. Then, there was the poetry of Donne whose 'Go and catch a falling star' he set to music: 'your Dr Donne' Elizabeth was to call the poet whom Ben Jonson had called 'the first poet in the world in some things', though – significantly, 'through not being understood he would perish.' But before Donne came more immediate influences.

In 1821 Keats, aged twenty-five, had died of consumption in Rome, and in the following year Shelley, not quite thirty, was drowned while sailing near Pisa. Young Browning had never heard of either, but Byron was another matter, for all the world heard of his death in 1824 during the Greek War of Independence against the Turks. So the twelve-year-old Browning read the romantic poetry of Byron, and it was probably this that inspired him to write a number of poems to which he gave the title *Incondita* – 'Crudities'. Crude some of them may have been, but he did not really think them so at the time, and both he and his parents were so pleased with them that they tried to find a publisher. They failed, of course, though there were other admirers, among them their friends the Flowers who lived in the village of Dalston on the other side of the Thames. Benjamin Flower was a former editor of the *Cambridge Intelligencer* who had spent six months in prison for publishing his advanced liberal views, and at this time was a widower with two daughters, Eliza and Sarah, some years older than Robert. They were remarkable young women, as gifted as they were beautiful, devoted to poetry, music and religion – Sarah wrote 'Nearer, my God, to Thee' – and when they read *Incondita* they made a copy for their album and sent two of the poems to their father's friend William Fox, a unitarian minister of neighbouring Finsbury. According to Browning, Fox praised his verses 'not a little', though he considered them to have 'too great splendour of language and too little wealth of thought', a criticism that he could scarcely make of his later work. In this way Browning met his 'literary godfather', the man who was to write the first review of his first published poem and help him to find a publisher for the second. Fox also became guardian of the Flower sisters when their father died in 1829, by which time Browning was recovering from his adolescent passion for Eliza. He had known the girls since childhood, and one cannot help wondering if they were the 'two wives' whom he married that Sunday morning when he was seven or eight years old.

Browning destroyed his manuscript when it failed to find a publisher, and after the death of the sisters twenty years later secured the destruction of their album copies, and the only poems to survive were the two, long lost, that they had sent to Fox.[4] They are both quite short, a hundred lines or so, and both highly 'Romantic', like the tales of Edgar Allan Poe and paintings of Fuseli: horror poems of plague, disaster, madness and death. *The First-Born of Egypt* is written in blank verse, remarkably accomplished and fluid verse for one so young, the lines more often than not flowing into one another without a pause:

> for 'twas a fearful thing
> To see a nation's hope so blasted. One
> Press'd his dead child unto his heart – no spot
> Of livid plague. . . .

Descriptive passages, particularly the opening one (apart from the simple, menacing first line) tend to be overloaded with adjectives, like most juvenile verse:

> That night came on in Egypt with a step
> So calmly stealing in the gorgeous train
> Of sunset glories flooding the pale clouds
> With liquid gold . . .

But the most interesting thing is that the poem is dramatic, a foretaste of the future, a dramatic monologue spoken by a witness of the last plague of Egypt: 'I sought the street to gaze upon the grief / Of congregated Egypt,' and there follows the moving description of the old, blind man who discovers that his only son and guide is dead, and the less satisfactory conclusion of the young chapel-goer, a tribute to 'Israel's God, whose red hand had avenged / His servants' cause so fearfully.

The Dance of Death, triumphant songs by Fever, Pestilence, Ague, Madness and Consumption, was obviously inspired by Coleridge's *Fire, Famine and*

Slaughter. Both are written in rhyme, in free octosyllabics, and each has a refrain, Browning's being 'Bow to me!' And Consumption, the dreaded nineteenth-century scourge that was to carry off the Flower sisters, has the last word: 'Bow to the deadliest – bow to me!' Few readers would attribute the poems, written with such confidence, to a boy of fourteen.

The boy was soon to come under an even more intoxicating influence than that of Byron. He left school in 1826, when only fourteen, and at about the same time his cousin James Silverthorne gave him a small volume of Shelley's lyrics. So excited was he by the poems that he covered their pages with his comments: 'foolish scribblings' he was to call them later, that showed 'the impression made on a boy by this first specimen of Shelley's poetry.' It followed that his mother bought for him all the works of Shelley that she could find, including, ironically enough, *Queen Mab*: ironically, because the devout Nonconformist was unwittingly presenting her son with 'Mr Shelley's atheistical poem'. Shelley himself was only eighteen when he wrote it, only four years older than Browning when he read this story of how the Fairy Queen flies in her chariot with the spirit of a sleeping girl to a celestial palace where (a remarkable anticipation of space-flight) 'The sun's unclouded orb / Rolled through the black concave,' and they can see the memorials and activities of man. Queen Mab explains: 'From kings, and priests, and statesmen, war arose,' and much of man's misery is the result of his belief in a God whose name 'Has fenced about all crimes with holiness.' But, 'There is no God,' and Shelley describes an ideal world of the future in which man loves man – and animals:

> no longer now
> He slays the lamb that looks him in the face,
> And horribly devours his mangled flesh,
> Which, still avenging Nature's broken law,
> Kindled all putrid humours in his frame,
> All evil passions, and all vain belief,
> Hatred, despair, and loathing in his mind,
> The germs of misery, death, disease, and crime.

Browning in his fifteenth year was at the stage of adolescent revolt against authority, even the so mild authority of adoring parents, and to show his independence proclaimed himself an atheist and vegetarian like Shelley. His vegetarianism lasted two years, but religious doubt was strengthened and prolonged by his discovery of Voltaire, and he so shook the faith of the Flower sisters that Sarah wrote to Mr Fox at the end of 1827:

The cloud has come over me gradually, and I did not discover the darkness in which my soul was shrouded until, in seeking to give light to others, my gloomy state became too settled to admit of doubt. It was in answering Robert Browning that my mind refused to bring forward argument, turned recreant, and sided with the enemy.

Meanwhile the boy continued his education at home. No doubt his father coached him, in an unorthodox and desultory fashion, in Latin and Greek, but tutors were engaged to teach him French and Italian. The celebrated John Relfe, musician to his Majesty, and a neighbour, helped him with his piano playing, and Isaac Nathan, who set Byron's *Hebrew Melodies* ('vile Ebrew nasalities' Byron called his compositions) was his singing-master. If only he had made the acquaintance of music's sister, mathematics, and learned something of modern science and scientific method, he might also have learned to express himself with greater concision and clarity in verse. As it was, for most of the time he was left to his own devices: the six thousand volumes of his father's library were at his command, and the Dulwich Gallery and London theatres only a few miles away. He was always fond of walking, but no gentleman's education was complete without instruction in other forms of physical activity, and riding and fencing were to be two main themes and sources of imagery in his poetry.

As a Nonconformist, Browning was virtually debarred from Oxford and Cambridge, but in 1828 London University was opened, and as there was no religious test he was one of its first students. His father entered him for Classics and German, and engaged a room for him in neighbouring Bedford Square, but the teaching was no more to his liking than had been that of Mr Ready's school. Nor did he like being away from home, and after little more than a week returned, which meant giving up his morning classes in German, and after little more than six months he abandoned the experiment altogether.

The trouble was that he lacked the discipline and loyalty that school might have given him; not the discipline imposed by flogging and bullying at the great public-schools, but the self-discipline and consideration for others that he should have learned at a good day-school. As it was, he was a clever, spoiled, conceited, impatient and aggressive adolescent. It was by no means altogether his own fault, however, and his sister was probably right when later she defended him at this stage: 'The fact was, poor boy, he had outgrown his social surroundings. They were absolutely good, but they were narrow; it could not be otherwise; he chafed under them.'

In May 1830 the boy was eighteen, almost a man, time that he decided how he was going to make a living. It was an eventful year. In July there was another revolution in France, when the restored and reactionary Bourbons were over-thrown and replaced by a 'Citizen King', Louis Philippe. Although the fighting in Paris had been done by the workers, the revolt was controlled by the bourgeoisie, with whom the English middle-class naturally sympathised, and by whom they were encouraged to stage their own milder, constitutional revolution in November, when Wellington's Tory government was defeated by the Whigs pledged to reform. But before this, in September, the railway era had begun, when the Duke attended the opening of the Manchester and Liverpool Railway and the locomotive claimed its first vicitm, William Huskisson, who was knocked down, and died while being carried to hospital at the unbelievable speed of 36 miles an hour.

But young Browning had no wish to become an engine-driver or an engineer, nor was he greatly interested in politics and reform. He might have become a clerk in the Bank of England like his father and grandfather, but Mr Browning, who endured rather than enjoyed his work, would scarcely recommend that for his son. There remained the three main professions worthy of a gentleman: the Church, the Army and the Law. But the boy was not a member of the Church of England, not even a practising Nonconformist, but an atheist still struggling with his doubts. Nor did the life of a soldier, inevitably for the greater part of the time divorced from books, appeal to him. He was interested in law, or rather, in the motives that led men to break it; but a barrister's training was a long one; the boy really wanted to write, not prose but verse, and to this his indulgent father agreed, even though the prospect of making a living out of poetry was bleak, and it meant supporting him for an indefinite period. So young Browning prepared to make writing his career, and as prelude to his work sat down and read the two folio volumes of Johnson's *Dictionary*. Yet even as late as the autumn of 1832 he appears to have been undecided, for he was later to write: 'I don't know whether I had not made up my mind to *act* as well as to make verses, music, and God knows what.'

The occasion was when, on 22 October, he had walked the ten miles to Richmond, probably with his cousin James, to see Edmund Kean play in *Richard III*, not exactly Shakespeare's, but Colley Cibber's more than century-old popular patchwork of speeches culled from half-a-dozen of the Histories, with improvements of his own invention. However, the combination of Kean, Cibber and Shakespeare so moved the young man that he conceived the idea of writing an anonymous poem, novel, opera and so on, the bewildered world never to know that they were the work of the same hand. First of the series was to be the poem, and by the following January he had written the thousand lines of *Pauline: A Fragment of a Confession*. He did not tell his parents, and it was his aunt Mrs Silverthorne who paid £30 for publication of the anonymous poem, which appeared in March 1833.

Like Wordsworth's *Prelude*, it is autobiography in verse, a brief account of the first twenty years of Browning's life, and a confession of how he lost the religious faith that he had only just regained: a confession to 'Pauline', possibly Eliza Flower. 'If, in spite of his denials, any woman inspired *Pauline*,' wrote Mrs Sutherland Orr, his first biographer, who knew him swell, 'it can have been no other than she.' Yet if it were, it was Eliza idealised, for there is nothing that we know of in their relationship to suggest the passion of the opening lines: 'Pauline, mine own, bend o'er me – thy soft breast / Shall pant to mine. . . .'

Confession was a favourite theme of the romantic poets, and *Pauline* is a romantic poem, as might be expected of a young man who was a devotee of Shelley and Byron: romantic not only in matter but also in manner, as in the use of the archaic second person singular: 'thy soft breast', 'thou art gone'. But Browning was not really a romantic poet. It is true that he liked the sensational and macabre, and in that sense was a romantic; but he was an extrovert not an introvert, his genius essentially dramatic, the exploration of the minds and motives of others, not the revelation of his own. His development was to be towards a greater and greater realism, and Lippo Lippi, Bishop Blougram, Mr Sludge, Guido Franceschini and the characters in *The Inn Album* talk like real men and women, not like poetic fabrications. Pauline is not a real woman like Andrea del Sarto's Lucrezia, though neither speaks, and the self-denigration – 'Oh Pauline, I am ruined' – is the morbid delight of a young man in his trivial failures, rather than the genuine grief of the older man that he would have the reader believe him to be: 'As life wanes, all its care and strife and toil / Seem strangely valueless.'

But the main fault of the poem is its lapses into obscurity, like a moon-flooded landscape masked by drifting clouds, and too often the reader is baffled by pronouns with ambiguous antecedents, and loses himself in a wilderness of relative clauses and parentheses. Yet it is comparatively clear as a whole. First, the early influence of his father's books, of Homer and the Greek dramatists, which left a feeling that their spirit dwelt in him. Yet,

> My life has not been that of those whose heaven
> Was lampless save where poesy shone out;
> But as a clime where glittering mountain-tops
> And glancing sea and forests steeped in light

> Give back reflected the far-flashing sun;
> For music (which is earnest of a heaven,
> Seeing we know emotions strange by it,
> Not else to be revealed), is like a voice,
> A low voice calling fancy, as a friend,
> To the green woods in the gay summer time:
> And she fills all the way with dancing shapes
> Which have made painters pale, and they go on
> Till stars look at them and winds call to them
> As they leave life's path for the twilight world
> Where the dead gather.

Music, painting and the stars run like three threads throughout the poem.

As a boy, he saw God everywhere, but then came the discovery of Shelley, the Sun-treader who inspired him with a belief in man: 'Men were to be as gods and earth as heaven.' But it did not last:

> First went my hopes of perfecting mankind,
> Next – faith in them, and then in freedom's self
> And virtue's self, then my own motives, ends
> And aims and loves, and human love went last.

And God was also gone, leaving him restless, selfish, envious, hating rather than loving, yet with a hunger after God. But eventually he rediscovered his faith, beauty rose on him again, and the poem ends triumphantly,

> Sun-treader, I believe in God and truth
> And love. . . .
> Know my last state is happy, free from doubt
> Or touch of fear. Love me and wish me well.

Pauline is interesting autobiographically, as a young poet's spiritual progress, even though the feelings are inflated, the remorse exaggerated; yet he must have felt a genuine sense of guilt at his desertion of his devout, devoted mother, whom, oddly enough, he does not mention. But even more interesting is the promise of the poetry. There are memorable lines:

> The morning swallows with their songs like words.

> secure some god
> To save will come in thunder from the stars.

> It joins its parent-river with a shout.

And there are equally memorable passages, notably those of the Sun-treader and the description of the distant country to which he would carry Pauline – not so very far from Camberwell!

Robert Browning

> Hedgerows for me – those living hedgerows where
> The bushes close and clasp above and keep
> Thought in.

The twenty-year-old author knew little about publishers, reviewers and the world of letters, but he knew the guardian of the Flower sisters, William Fox, although he had not met him since he was a boy, and as Fox was now editor of the *Monthly Repository* he wrote to him:

Dear Sir, – Perhaps by the aid of the subjoined initials and a little reflection, you may recollect an oddish sort of boy, who had the honour of being introduced to you at Hackney some years back – at that time a sayer of verse and a doer of it . . .: that individual it is who takes the liberty of addressing one whose slight commendation then, was more thought of than all the gun drum and trumpet of praise would be now, and to submit to you a free and easy sort of thing which he wrote some months ago 'on one leg' and which comes out this week. . . .

R.B.

As Fox agreed to consider the poem, Browning sent him twelve copies in the hope that he would distribute them among other periodicals, and shortly after the appearance of *Pauline* the anonymous reviewer of the anonymous poet pronounced his opinion. It was favourable, though not altogether ingenuous:

Whoever the anonymous author may be, he is a poet. . . . We felt certain of Tennyson . . .; we are not less certain of the author of *Pauline* . . . there are a few passages rather obscure, 'but that's not much.' In recognising a poet we cannot stand upon trifles. . . .

Browning wrote to Fox at once: 'I shall never write a line without thinking of the source of my first praise, be assured.'

In the *Athenaeum* Allan Cunningham wrote generously of the poet who sang as naturally and easily as a bird, but one of the few other periodicals that noticed the poem dismissed it as 'unfit for publication', while for another it was 'a piece of pure bewilderment'. This anticipated, and therefore precluded, a review that John Stuart Mill – a young man whose education had been not unlike Browning's – had written in his copy of the poem:

With considerable poetic powers, the writer seems to me possessed with a more intense and morbid self-consciousness than I ever knew in any sane human being. . . . I even question whether part even of that self-disdain is not *assumed*. He is evidently *dissatisfied*, and feels part of the badness of his state; he does not write as if it were purged out of him. If he once could muster a hearty hatred of his selfishness it would *go*; as it is, he feels only the lack of *good*, not the positive evil. He feels not remorse, but only disappointment. . . .

1. The Bank of England in the early nineteenth century, where Browning's father worked; it was a few miles north of Camberwell. Engraving by T. H. Shepherd. *Copyright British Museum.*

2. Dulwich Art Gallery—'That gallery I so love and am so grateful to'—built 1811–14 by Sir John Soane. *Courtesy Alleyn's College of God's Gift.*

So, these fellows say I've no
genius for Epic Poetry! — ~~They~~
advise me to attempt
Tragedy — they think, I
suppose I was 'prentice to
a Butcher — No! — & to shew
the utter contempt I have
for them — I'll return to farmer
Gubbins & keep pigs again!

3. Drawing by Browning's father. *Victoria & Albert Museum.*

Mill returned the book to Fox, who gave it to Browning, and as the young poet read the deep analysis of his secret self – 'self-seeking and self-worshipping' – he writhed and vowed never again thus to reveal his soul to others; that in future his poetry should be dramatic, the speech of imaginary characters, not of Robert Browning.

2. *From Success to Failure*

1834-40

VERY few copies of *Pauline* were sold, which was just as well, for Browning wanted to forget his Confession and, as it had been issued anonymously, it was not difficult to conceal his authorship from the world. But it was not until the end of October, seven months after publication, that he read Mill's penetrating criticism, and by that time he was far into another poem: the subject Sordello, a medieval troubadour, to whom he had been introduced by his Italian tutor, and about whom he had read in his father's *Biographie Universelle*. Mill's strictures, therefore, in addition to hurting his pride, made him reread what he had written, and begin to revise, cutting or altering passages that might be interpreted as further revelations of the soul of Robert Browning, and it must have been with relief that at the beginning of 1834 he accepted an invitation to go to Russia. It may have been his uncle Reuben Browning who introduced him to the Russian Consul General, suggesting that his nephew might accompany him on a mission to St Petersburg, nominally as his secretary. In any event, they started at the beginning of March, and from Rotterdam drove east and north along the line of the Baltic into the seemingly endless, snow-covered forests that led to the Russian capital. There they stayed long enough to see the break-up of the ice on the Neva, and the Czar perform the annual ceremony of drinking a glass of water from the river. Browning's letters written during this journey have been lost, but he was to recall it forty years later when writing *Ivàn Ivànovitch:*

> ... verst and verst of pine,
> From village to village runs the road's long wide bare line.
> Clearance and clearance break the else-unconquered growth
> Of pine and all that breeds and broods there. ...

He was back in Camberwell in time for his twenty-second birthday in May – it is easy to forget how young he was – when he resumed the uncongenial task of revising what he had written of *Sordello*. But his Russian journey had revived an early interest in diplomacy and the possibility of a diplomatic career, so much so that he applied for a post with a mission that was to go to Persia, though he was not sorry to hear that it had been filled when he heard that the October temperature in Bagdad was 127 in the shade. It was now that he made the acquaintance of an agent of the deposed Bourbons, the Comte Amédée de Ripert-Monclar, again probably through his uncle Reuben, for both were associated with the great international banking house of the Rothschilds. Acquaintance rapidly developed into friendship, and when Browning told his new friend something of his difficulties with *Sordello*, it was he who suggested as a possible subject for another poem the story of Paracelsus. As Browning already knew something of the life of Paracelsus, he accepted the suggestion with alacrity, and abandoned the medieval troubadour in favour of the Renaissance physician, one of the pioneers of modern science, who rejected a pedantic scholasticism and crippling authority of the Church for the study of nature.

Theophrastus Bombast von Hohenheim was born near Zurich about 1490, and as a young man assumed the name of Paracelsus to assert his claim that he was the equal of Celsus, the famous Roman physician and author of *De Medicina*. Browning himself appended to his poem a brief life of his hero, taken from the *Biographie Universelle*, and written by no friendly hand:

... Paracelsus travelled among the mountains of Bohemia, in the East and in Sweden ... everywhere communicating freely, not merely with the physicians, but the old women, charlatans and conjurers. ...

At about the age of thirty-three, many astonishing cures which he wrought on eminent personages procured him such a celebrity, that he was called in 1526 to fill a chair of physic and surgery at the University of Basil. There Paracelsus began by burning publicly in the amphitheatre the works of Avicenna and Galen, assuring his auditors that the latchets of his shoes were more instructed than those two physicians. ...

But at Basil it was speedily perceived that the new Professor was no better than an egregious quack. ... According to the testimony of Oporinus, who lived two years in his intimacy, Paracelsus scarcely ever ascended the lecture-desk unless half drunk. ...

At length ... he fled from Basil towards the end of the year 1527, and ... entered once more upon the career of ambulatory theosophist ... Paracelsus proceeded to Salzburg, where he died in the Hospital of St Stephen, Sept. 24, 1541.

Browning wrote his poem in the six or seven months between the early autumn of 1834 and spring of 1835, when Fox helped him to find a publisher, who issued it in August at his father's expense. It can be considered either as a dramatic poem in five parts or as a closet drama in five acts, for its length, 4000

33

lines, lack of action and of characters other than Paracelsus preclude performance. There are only three other characters, and they speak little, or relatively little: the girl Michal, her lover Festus, and the poet Aprile.

The story begins in the autumn of 1510, when Paracelsus, aged twenty-two like Browning, is saying good-bye to his friends Festus and Michal in a walled Würzburg garden, not unlike that of Hanover Cottage, Camberwell, with its crickets, lizards and spiders, in the autumn of 1834. In *Pauline* Browning had confessed his craving after knowledge, and this is the theme of *Paracelsus*: he too, 'will KNOW'. But his quest is not in the service of mankind; if he can serve them incidentally, "Tis well, but there our intercourse must end.' Festus warns him of the danger of neglecting human love, but Paracelsus sets out confidently:

> to KNOW
> Rather consists in opening out a way
> Whence the imprisoned splendour may escape,
> Than in effecting entry for a light
> Supposed to be without.

Nine years later Paracelsus, prematurely aged, is in Constantinople. He feels that he has failed, and is wondering if he has been mistaken in his search for knowledge at the expense of love, when he meets the poet Aprile. 'I am he that aspired to KNOW: and thou?' he asks; and Aprile replies, 'I would *love* infinitely, and be loved.' The one has knowledge and power without love, the other love and beauty without knowledge. But such love is not enough, it is selfish as the quest for knowledge; the lover must know, and the knower must love. Aprile dies, and Paracelsus sets out again with the words: 'Let me love! I have attained.'

Another five years, and Paracelsus is a professor at Basel, trying to impart his knowledge to students and fellow scholars for whom, in spite of his attempt to love, he feels little but contempt. Utterly miserable, he has failed again:

> Love, hope, fear, faith – these make humanity;
> These are its sign and note and character,
> And these I have lost!

He must *know*.

Two years later, expelled from Basel by his jealous opponents as 'a most egregious quack', he is drinking at an inn when he explains to Festus that though his aim is the same, his method has changed:

> I seek to know and to enjoy at once,
> Not one without the other as before.

Half-drunk, he admits that the whole plan is a makeshift, though it will last his time, and asks Festus if he does not scorn him for his self-deceit. But when he hears that Michal is dead, he resolves to perish in a last attempt to achieve his aim.

Last scene of all is a hospital cell in 1541. The dying Paracelsus rises from his bed, puts on his academic robes and, as the mouthpiece of God, addresses Festus. Progress, he says, is the law of life, and man, yet in his infancy, will at last attain perfection. But he must love as well as strive for knowledge and power. Aprile's failure,

> love's undoing
> Taught me the worth of love in man's estate,
> And what proportion love should hold with power
> In his right constitution; love preceding
> Power, and with much power, always much more love. . . .
> All this I knew not, and I failed. Let men
> Regard me, and the poet dead long ago
> Who loved too rashly; and shape forth a third
> And better tempered spirit, warned by both.

When Browning wrote those words in March 1835 he could not be aware that another young man who desired to KNOW, a naturalist on board H.M.S. *Beagle*, was sailing up the coast of Chile on his way to the Galapagos Archipelago. His name was Charles Darwin, and there, at about the time of publication of *Paracelsus*, he conceived the idea that was to lead to the *Origin of Species* and *Descent of Man*. 'Man in his arrogance thinks himself a great work worthy the interposition of a deity,' he noted. 'More humble and I believe truer to consider him created from animals.' A very different conception of man's history from that of Paracelsus-Browning.

Nevertheless, *Paracelsus* is an uncommonly good and original poem, though it will probably never be a popular one, for it would have been even better had it been shorter, more concentrated, and therefore easier for the reader himself to concentrate and follow. The trouble was that Browning thought that the business of poetry was to teach, as twenty years later he was to write to Ruskin:

Is the business of it to tell people what they know already . . .? It is all teaching, on the contrary, and the people hate to be taught. They say otherwise – make foolish fables about Orpheus enchanting stocks and stones, poets standing up and being worshipped – all nonsense and impossible dreaming. A poet's affair is with God, to whom he is accountable, and of whom is his reward.

Yet Shakespeare (or more probably Fletcher) wrote the lyric 'Orpheus with his lute', and Shelley's affair was scarcely with God, nor was that of Housman, who wrote, 'Poetry is not the thing said, but a way of saying it.' Of course the poet teaches, may teach, incidentally, but the proper medium for didacticism is prose, and the poetry does not lie in the teaching, but in the words, their music and multitudinous associations:

As when a queen, long dead, was young.

The line is Browning's, sung by Paracelsus, and these eight simple English monosyllables are perhaps the most memorable in the whole poem.

Fortunately Browning often forgot, or neglected, his mission to teach, and then he wrote the songs in *Paracelsus* and lines of blank verse such as:

Lakes which, when morn breaks on their quivering bed,
Blaze like a wyvern flying round the sun,

in which the initial reversed beat of 'Blaze like', followed by the juxtaposed assonantal trochaic words 'wyvern flying', imposes a falling rhythm on the basic rising one. But technically, and musically, Browning's blank verse is not remarkable, partly because he failed to exploit a final redundant syllable for the same purpose, so that such a line-ending as 'No ancient hunter lifted' is exceptional.

Pauline had been published anonymously, and *Paracelsus* was the first work to carry the name of Robert Browning on its title-page. Fox reviewed it well, but not enthusiastically: it was a work of thought, skill and toil, but would bear condensation, and gain in clarity by the avoidance of amplification and repetition. Other reviews found it dreamy and obscure, with 'elements of tediousness'. Leigh Hunt praised its originality, but warned the author 'to beware of being seduced, while seeking to produce new and bold effects, into either slovenliness or affectation.' But the most encouraging review was an unsigned one in the *Examiner* by a young man of exactly Browning's age, John Forster:

He [the reader] will find enough of beauty to compensate for the tedious passages, were they ten times as obscure and tedious. . . . It is some time since we read a work of more unequivocal power than this. We conclude that its author is a young man. . . . If so, we may safely predict for him a brilliant career, if he continues true to the present promise of his genius. He possesses all the elements of a fine poet.

In spite of Forster's enthusiastic review and the more cautiously favourable ones of Fox and Hunt, *Paracelsus* was a financial failure for Browning's father, though for the author it was a literary and social triumph, for it brought him into touch with the world of letters and made him many influential friends.

One of these, and most important at the time, was William Macready. When Edmund Kean died, six months after Browning had seen him play Richard III, Macready had become the leading tragedian of the day, and on 27 November 1835 the middle-aged actor met the youthful poet. That evening Macready was dining with Fox at his Bayswater home, when Browning called. 'His face is full of intelligence,' Macready noted, and before parting they had agreed to meet again, and Browning promised to send him a copy of *Paracelsus*. A week later Macready read the poem, 'a work of great daring, starred with poetry of thought, feeling, and diction, but occasionally obscure; the writer can scarcely fail to be a leading spirit of his time.' So impressed was he both by the poet and the poem, that he invited Browning to a New-Year's Eve party at his country house at Elstree, some miles north of London. The journey was made by coach, and among the passengers was another young man who was also going to the party, though they did not speak until they were introduced by their host: 'Mr Browning – Mr Forster.' 'Did you see a little notice of you I wrote in the *Examiner*?' Forster asked; and another friendship had begun. There were others. 'Mr. Browning was very popular with the whole party,' Macready wrote in his Diary; 'his simple and enthusiastic manner engaged attention, and won opinions from all present; he looks and speaks more like a youthful poet than any man I ever saw.' Among these new friends was Macready's neighbour, Fanny Haworth, and it was either she or Macready who introduced him to Harriet Martineau, ten years his senior, and author of simple stories illustrating the abuses of the age.

Browning's friendship with Macready had inevitably turned his thoughts to writing for the theatre, and in February 1836, after seeing him play Othello, he and Forster called to discuss the plot of a tragedy that he had in mind, the subject a characteristically obscure one: Narses, a sixth-century Armenian eunuch and soldier in the service of Rome. Narses was to be abandoned, but meanwhile Forster had written an article called 'Evidences of a New Genius for Dramatic Poetry', which was published in the March number of the *New Monthly Magazine*:

... Without the slightest hesitation we name Mr Robert Browning at once with Shelley, Coleridge, Wordsworth ... a man of genius, he has in himself all the elements of a great poet, philosophical as well as dramatic ... startlingly original ... power of a great dramatic poet; we never think of Mr Browning while we read his poem; we are not identified with him, but with the persons into whom he has flung his genius.

No wonder Browning was thinking of writing for the stage.

Then on 26 May came the famous dinner-party given by Thomas Talfourd, recently created Serjeant-at-Law, and author of the tragedy *Ion* which had just been successfully produced with Macready in the title role. Among the guests were Miss Mitford, author of *Our Village*, and Wordsworth, Crabb Robinson and Landor, all of whom Browning then met for the first time. There were toasts: Macready proposed Talfourd, Talfourd proposed Macready, and added another to the Poets of England, including Robert Browning. Although Wordsworth was sitting opposite Browning, the anecdote that the old poet leaned across the table and said 'I am proud to drink to your health, Mr Browning,' is probably apocryphal, for Crabb Robinson did not mention Browning in his Diary. After the speeches conversation became general, and Macready lightly remarked to Miss Mitford that the occasion should encourage her to write a play. 'Will you act in it?' she asked. Macready made no reply, but as Browning was leaving the house he said: 'Write a play, Browning, and keep me from going to America.'

Two days later Browning wrote to say that when he had finished *Sordello* he would give his 'whole heart and soul to the writing a Tragedy', and on 3 August Macready wrote in his Diary: 'Forster told me that Browning had fixed on Strafford for the subject of a tragedy; he could not have hit upon one that I could have more readily concurred in.' It was to be another three years before *Sordello* was completed, but meanwhile there was good reason why he should have chosen Strafford as a subject, for Forster had been taken ill while writing an account of his life, and Browning had helped him to finish it in time for publication. Macready received the manuscript of the play, though not quite complete, in the middle of November, and was greatly pleased with it, but when he began to read it again '*very attentively*' he found that he had been 'too much carried away by the truth of character to observe the meanness of plot, and occasional obscurity.' Browning took his script away for revision, and it was not until the end of March 1837 that he brought it back. On the following day, the manager of Covent Garden Theatre heard the play read and was so pleased that he agreed to produce it without delay, though Macready still had his doubts: it was 'too historical'. He and Forster made alterations and, not unnautrally, there was a squabble with Browning, who himself made changes in the last scene; 'found them quite bad,' wrote Macready, 'mere feeble rant . . . it must fail.'

However, the play was produced successfully on 1 May 1837, with Macready as Strafford, John Vandenhoff as Pym, and Helen Faucit, then little more than a girl, as Lady Carlisle. Reviews in the next morning's papers were on the whole favourable. Although obscure, unintelligible to those who did not know their history of Charles I, the language was spirited and dramatic, and the author had avoided 'mere poetry'. *The Times*, too, found it *very* historical, and probably unintelligible to most people, complained that the number of broken sentences made it difficult to understand (other reviewers agreed), but concluded that the play was one of no little promise. It ran for another three nights, and a fifth performance was announced for the 11th, but Vandenhoff had had enough after reading that he was 'sadly prosy in Pym', and, apart from a benefit performance and one or two antiquarian revivals later in the century, that was the end of *Strafford* on the stage. It was published, however, and not at the author's expense, on the day of the first performance, and dedicated to Macready 'by his most grateful and devoted friend, R.B.'

Browning took up the story of Thomas Wentworth towards the end of his career, when he returned from Ireland in 1639, and was created Earl of Strafford. Originally a supporter of Eliot and Pym in their struggle against Charles I's personal misgovernment, he had changed sides and become the King's principal supporter, and the tragedy is Pym's relentless pursuit of his old friend, who is betrayed by the vacillating Charles and executed in 1641. It is a splendid theme, but Browning failed to make much of it. It *is* too historical for an average audience, and the young dramatist, unlike the young Shakespeare, seems incapable of saying a plain thing plainly; his characters talk in hints: 'What can he mean?' asks Lady Carlisle; 'What can you mean?' asks Charles, and the reader impatiently asks the same question. Partly because of this haziness of speech we cannot take much interest in any of the characters, and the most affecting episode is the simple one at the beginning of the last scene, where Strafford is talking to his children in the Tower:

> And faint, and fainter, and then all's quite gone,
> Music and light and all, like a lost star,

says his little son after singing an Italian song. Lady Carlisle uses the same image, with a difference, earlier in the play: 'Well, when the eve has its last streak / The night has its first star.' The star image was a favourite one with Browning, Strafford himself employing it twice in consecutive lines; and equally characteristic is the reference to a woman's hair, when Strafford wearily turns from thoughts of his friendly enemy to say irrelevantly to Lady Carlisle, 'Child, your hair / Is glossier than the Queen's!'

Browning was too much interested in motive, too little in action to make a successful dramatist, and in his Preface himself described *Strafford* as a play of

'Action in Character, rather than Character in Action'. But he added that he had 'a jaded mind' when he wrote it – Macready noted that a month before its production he looked 'very unwell, jaded and thought-sick' – and he did not despair of writing a successful play. Meanwhile, he put *Strafford* on one side, tried to forget it, like *Pauline*, and twelve years later excluded it from the first collected edition of his work.

Yet, even before he began to write *Strafford*, Fox had published in his *Monthly Repository* of January 1836 two short poems by 'Z' that showed where his true genius lay: the dramatic monologue. Both described abnormal states of mind, so that when they were published together in the *Dramatic Lyrics* of 1842 it was under the joint title 'Madhouse Cells'. One was the satirical-compassionate *Johannes Agricola*, the meditation of one of Martin Luther's pupils who became an Antinomian, maintaining that the elect are saved by grace and not by observance of any moral law:

> For as I lie, smiled on, full-fed
> With unexhausted blessedness,
> I gaze below on hell's fierce bed,
> And those its waves of flame oppress,
> Swarming in ghastly wretchedness;
> Whose life on earth aspired to be
> One altar-smoke, so pure!

Even better is the soliloquy of the crazy lover who secures his mistress by murdering her. He sits beside her, his head on her white shoulder:

> That moment she was mine, mine, fair,
> Perfectly pure and good: I found
> A thing to do, and all her hair
> In one long yellow string I wound
> Three times her little throat around,
> And strangled her. . . .
> And thus we sit together now,
> And all night long we have not stirred,
> And yet God has not said a word!

Brief, concentrated, lucid in spite of its crazy speaker, *Porphyria's Lover* is first of the dramatic monologues that go to make Browning one of the most original, one of the greatest, poets in the English language.

He celebrated his twenty-fifth birthday during the short run of *Strafford* at Covent Garden, and Fox's little daughter 'Tottie', later Mrs Bridell-Fox, had a vivid memory of him at this time:

I remember ... when Mr Browning entered the drawing-room, with a quick light step; and on hearing from me that my father was out, and in fact that nobody was at home but myself, he said: 'It's my birthday to-day; I'll wait till they come in,' and sitting down to the piano, he added: 'If it won't disturb you, I'll play till they do.' ... He was then slim and dark, and very handsome; and – may I hint it – just a trifle of a dandy, addicted to lemon-coloured kid-gloves and such things: quite 'the glass of fashion and the mould of form.' But full of ambition, eager for success, eager for fame, and, what's more, determined to conquer fame and to achieve success.

It is a lively portrait of the fortunate young man, author of a long successful poem, ambitious and self-confident, recently become the friend or acquaintance of many distinguished men and women, and for the first time earning money by the production of his play with England's most famous actor in the lead. And then, he had another long poem on the verge of completion: 'Nearly ready, Sordello, in Six Books,' his publishers had announced in their week-old edition of *Strafford*. Yet it was to be nearly three years before *Sordello* appeared.

In June William IV died, and was succeeded by his eighteen-year-old niece. The long Victorian Age that was to outlast Browning and the nineteenth century had begun.

It began badly for Browning. In July Mrs W. Busk published her *Plays and Poems*, one of them being 'Sordello', a poem in Six Books, and the *Athenaeum* asked, 'Is this founded upon the same subject as that chosen by the author of "Paracelsus" for his announced poem?' It was, and it told much the same story that Browning, with intervals for the writing of *Paracelsus* and *Strafford*, had spent four years in telling. He had already written two versions of *Sordello*, the second being his drastic revision of the original poem made after reading Mill's penetrating analysis of *Pauline* as a revelation of the author's soul. This second version treated Sordello's story more objectively, more dramatically, and instead of invoking the spirit of Shelley again, he told the Sun-treader that this time he must not come near. The story was to be 'the progress of a soul', but written in such a way that it could not be interpreted as the progress of Robert Browning's soul. Now, after the publication of Mrs Busk's poem, he began a second revision, or third version, to which he added a more detailed historical background. Then, having worked at this for some months, he decided to go to Italy to see the places about which he was writing, Venice and its neighbourhood, and in April 1838 sailed from London as the only passenger in a merchant ship bound for Trieste.

The weather was stormy, and for the first fortnight he was very ill, but recovered sufficiently to witness the righting of a ship they found drifting keel upwards, full of smuggled goods and half-a-dozen decomposing corpses. He took two cutlasses and a dagger as souvenirs. By the time they reached Trieste the captain had grown so fond of him that he offered him a free passage to Constantinople and, on his declining, accepted a pair of gloves that he had worn on deck as a memento. Browning always wore gloves when out-of-doors; one thinks of the lemon-coloured kid-gloves of Miss Fox's recollection, and even when an old man posing for a photograph outside his front door, he wore gloves.

It is important to understand the political situation in Italy at this time: that it was not a united country like France, but a number of small independent states under foreign rulers. Across the centre, with its capital at Rome, ran the broad belt of the Papal States governed by the Pope. South of this was the Kingdom of the Two Sicilies ruled from Naples by a degenerate branch of the Spanish Bourbons, while to the north Venetia and Lombardy were part of the Austrian Empire. There were Austrian rulers, too, in the Duchies of Tuscany, Modena and Parma, and, apart from the Papal States, the only province of Italy ruled by an Italian was the Kingdom of Piedmont (or Sardinia) with its capital at Turin in the north-west. When, therefore, Browning arrived at Trieste at the head of the Adriatic in May 1839 he landed in the Austrian Empire, and the whole of his Italian tour was in Austrian territory.

However, he was not concerned with contemporary Italian history, but with that of six centuries earlier, the period of Sordello and warring city-states, when Guelph fought Ghibelline (really German 'Welf' and 'Waiblingen'), supporters respectively of the Papacy and so-called Holy Roman (but really German) Empire, when Florence fought Siena, and Crema neighbouring Cremona. From Trieste Browning went to Venice, from which he made an excursion through Treviso and Bassano to 'delicious Asolo' on the foothills of the Alps – 'all my places and castles' – then back through Vicenza and Padua to Venice. His journey home took him west again, to Verona, then north over the Alps to Munich, down the Rhine to Cologne, and so to Antwerp and back to London at the end of July.

He was now ready to begin his fourth and final version of *Sordello*, and at this he worked for nearly a year, until the early summer of 1839. This involved the addition of more historical detail and description of scenery, of a newly awakened sympathy for the poor and oppressed, a sympathy that had to be imparted to his hero, who thus became their champion and a supporter of the more liberal Guelph faction, and finally, Sordello's discovery that his father was the great warrior-prince of the north, Salinguerra – a Ghibelline.

'*Sordello*. By Robert Browning' was published – at his father's expense – in March 1840.

The real Sordello, as far as is known, was born in Mantua about the year 1200. He became the most famous of Italian troubadours, makers and singers of songs of courtly love, but first appears in a tavern brawl in Florence. When at the court of Verona, he carried off his master's wife, as a result of which he had to fly to Provence where, after various adventures, he died at about the age of seventy. The story was idealised and romanticised by Dante and others, whose works Browning read, and eventually the troubadour emerged as the young hero of his poem.

In outline, Browning's version of Sordello's story is simple enough. The Ghibelline Eccelino is driven from his city of Vicenza, and with him his wife Adelaide and infant son, saved by the archer Elcorte. His ally Salinguerra, lord of Ferrara, is also expelled, though he is less fortunate, for his wife dies after giving birth to Sordello, whom his father thinks also dead. To prevent future rivalry between the two boys, Adelaide brings up Sordello as her page in remote Goito, telling him that he is the son of Elcorte. There, he finds that he has a gift for poetry, and defeats the famous troubadour Eglamor in a contest, though he finds the conventional courtly poetry a form too narrow for his genius. He falls in love with Adelaide's daughter Palma, who persuades him to go with her to see Salinguerra at Ferrara, where she reveals that the fierce old warrior is the young poet's father. Palma's love and his father's power are now both his if he will take them, but they are Ghibellines, while he has come to think the Guelph cause that of the people, and poetry far more important than political power. He goes into another room to decide which to accept, and in the struggle between the worldly and the ideal, 'The Poet thwarting hopelessly the Man', he dies – like Shelley, at the age of thirty.

That is simple enough, but as told by Browning in 6000 lines of heroic verse, Sordello's story is not always easy to follow. Of course the fact that it was seven years in the making, and that during those years there was much re-writing, alteration and addition, is partly responsible for its frequent obscurity. Then, as he wrote twenty-three years later, when he dedicated the poem to Joseph Milsand, 'my stress lay on the incidents in the development of a soul: little else is worth study.' As a result, there is very little action, and description of that little is often so compressed as to be barely intelligible. There is no comedy, and almost the only relief for the reader is description of the scene, which Browning, although in pursuit of a soul, happily could not resist; Goito, for example:

> Goito; just a castle built amid
> A few low mountains; firs and larches hid
> Their main defiles, and rings of vineyard bound
> The rest. Some captured creature in a pound,
> Whose artless wonder quite precludes distress,
> Secure beside in its own loveliness,
> So peered with airy head, below, above,
> The castle at its toils, the lapwings love
> To glean among at grape-time.

But the main difficulty is in the writing itself: the idiosyncratic syntax, hints, half-hints, ambiguities, lacunae, inversions, parentheses, recondite allusions and confusing detail. It is as though, like Sordello's, Browning's

> argument dropped flat
> Through his accustomed fault of breaking yoke,
> Disjoining him who felt from him who spoke.

No doubt, had we but world enough and time, we could puzzle out the meaning of every page, and there are a few readers, like Rossetti and Ezra Pound, whose minds are so attuned to Browning's that they find no difficulty; but for the great majority it is difficult to concentrate on reams of writing such as this, taken at random from Sordello's last interminable soliloquy:

> Give
> Body and spirit the first right they claim,
> And pasture soul on a voluptuous shame
> That you, a pageant-city's denizen,
> Are neither vilely lodged midst Lombard men –
> Can force joy out of sorrow, seem to truck
> Bright attributes away for sordid muck,
> Yet manage from that very muck educe
> Gold; then subject, nor scruple, to your cruce
> The world's discardings!

After all, the most famous story of a soul in all literature is *Hamlet*, and if we compare the hundred lines or so of Hamlet's soliloquies with the hundreds of Sordello's the concentrated clarity of the one throws into even deeper shade the diffuse obscurity of the other. No wonder Elizabeth Barrett wrote five years later:

It is like a noble picture with its face to the wall just now – or at least, in the shadow. .... And such a work as it might become if you chose, if you put your will to it! What I meant to say yesterday was .. that (to my mind) it wants drawing together and fortifying in the connections and associations, which hang as loosely every here and there as those in a dream, and confound the reader who persists in thinking himself awake.

Browning was considering a revision with additional verses, but Elizabeth's advice was 'concentrate and clarify'. He was to learn much from her criticism. The pity is that it did not come sooner. If it had, he would have been saved the years of obscurity into which he sank with *Sordello*. For how right she was! 'Like a noble picture with its face to the wall – or at least, in the shadow.' For *Sordello* is so very nearly a great poem, might so easily – if that is not too easily said – have been one of the world's great poems, if only it had been moved into the light, made easier to see; if only all the writing had been as clear as that describing the effect of Palma's revelation to Salinguerra that Sordello is his son:

> On which ensued a strange
> And solemn visitation; there came change
> O'er every one of them; each looked on each:
> Up in the midst a truth grew, without speech.
> And when the giddiness sank and the haze
> Subsided, they were sitting, no amaze,
> Sordello with the baldric on, his sire
> Silent, though his proportions seemed aspire
> Momently; and, interpreting the thrill, –
> Night at its ebb, – Palma found there still
> Relating somewhat Adelaide confessed
> A year ago, while dying on her breast. . . .

There were one or two percipient reviews: 'full of gems set in puzzles . . . a promised land, spotted all over with disappointments, and yet most truly a land of promise, if ever so rich and rare a chaos can be developed into form and order by revision.' But for most critics the poem was a disastrous failure: 'hysterical and broken sobs of sentences'; 'digression, affectation, obscurity'; 'the impenetrable veil, both of manner and language'; 'a failure *in toto*'; 'trash of the very worst description'.

Even more galling than damning reviews was the poem's becoming a joke in literary circles. Tennyson professed to have understood only two lines, the first, 'Who will, may hear Sordello's story told,' and the last, 'Who would has heard Sordello's story told,' and they were both lies. (He cannot have read very carefully, for in the course of the story Browning desperately repeats the first line three times.) Douglas Jerrold, famous for his contributions to *Punch*, the first number of which appeared at this time, 1840, told how, when given a copy of the poem while recovering from an illness, he could not understand two consecutive lines, and thought he had gone mad. Less melodramatically, Harriet Martineau thought she must be ill when she tried to read it, and Mrs Carlyle professed to be unsure whether Sordello was a man, a city or a book.

Carlyle himself, who had come to like the young poet in spite of his dandyism, wrote a friendly letter, though he suggested that his next work might well be written in prose. Euphrasia Fanny Haworth, 'My English Eyebright' (*euphrasy*) of a parenthesis in the poem, also wrote encouragingly, and Browning replied, 'You say roses and lilies and lilac-bunches and lemon-flowers about it while everybody else pelts cabbage stump and potato-paring.'

Reviewers and ridicule had killed *Sordello*; sales averaged only ten a year, and Browning's reputation as a rising poet plunged like a plummet. It was a bad start to the decade of the forties.

3. The Unsuccessful Playwright

1840–45

THE decade of the 'Hungry Forties' was to be a momentous one for Britain and Europe as well as for Browning: of famine and rebellion in Ireland, revolution on the Continent, and in England of revolt, railway mania – and the penny post, which came in with *Sordello*. Exactly a year earlier the first number of 'Bradshaw's Railway Time Tables and Assistant to Railway Travelling' had appeared, price sixpence. There were then only 1200 miles of track in Britain, but by 1850 there were 7000, built by numerous competing companies who raised millions of pounds from the public, many of whom lost their savings in the financial crisis of 1847. A few days after the first issue of *Bradshaw* the Anti-Corn Law League was founded to demand the repeal of duties on imported grain, and in 1840 the National Charter Association for parliamentary reform: both in Manchester, a rapidly expanding city, but still unrepresented in Parliament. The Government replied by extending the newly-formed police force from London to the provinces; fortunately, for Sir Robert Peel's unarmed 'Bobbies' or 'Peelers' were popular, and there was no repetition of the 'Peterloo Massacre' of twenty years before.

In the world of literature, Coleridge and Scott had died in the 'thirties, and the seventy-year-old Wordsworth, now a platitudinous Tory instead of the fiery revolutionary poet that he had been at the turn of the century, was the only survivor of the great Romantics, and about to receive a government pension and succeed Southey as Poet Laureate, events that young Browning, now like his *Sordello* a champion of the people, was to deplore in 'The Lost Leader':

> Just for a handful of silver he left us,
>   Just for a riband to stick in his coat. . . .
> We that had loved him so, followed him, honoured him,
>   Lived in his mild and magnificent eye. . . .
> He alone breaks from the van and the freemen,
>   – He alone sinks to the rear and the slaves!

Among his contemporaries, Dickens, another champion of the people, had recently achieved fame with *Oliver Twist* and *Nicholas Nickleby*, and was about to start on a triumphant, unprecedented tour of the United States; and Thackeray was making his name with *Catherine, The Great Hoggarty Diamond,* and his contributions to *Punch,* including 'The Diary of C. Jeames de la Pluche Esq', a footman who made a fortune out of 'speculation in railroads'. Then, after a ten-year silence, the almost penniless Tennyson was preparing for publication the *Poems* that were to bring him recognition, fame – and a pension; and Elizabeth Barrett had just published *The Seraphim and other Poems,* for which she had been hailed as 'a genuine poetess of no common order'. She, too, was a humanitarian, and in 'The Cry of the Children' she exposed, as did Carlyle in *Past and Present,* the abuses of laissez-faire capitalism:

> For, all day, we drag our burden tiring,
> Through the coal-dark, underground –
> Or, all day, we drive the wheels of iron
> In the factories, round and round.

Perhaps the poem was partly responsible for the passing of the Mines Act of 1842 and Factory Act of 1844, the one forbidding employment of women and boys underground, the other of children under nine in factories.

So many of his contemporaries had achieved, or nearly achieved, success, but *Sordello* had plunged Browning into a semi-obscurity from which he was not to emerge for more than twenty years, and for many of the grand acquaintances that he had recently made he was merely a figure of fun. There were compensations, however. The Camberwell cottage had long been too small for Mr and Mrs Browning, their grown-up son Robert and daughter Sarianna, and ever-growing library, and in December 1840 they left it for a larger house and garden at New Cross, a mile or two farther east. This brought them into closer contact with the other branch of the Browning family, notably 'Uncle Reuben', who stabled with them the horse that his nephew used to exercise on weekdays. Then, if new acquaintances had been lost, old friends remained: William Fox, for example, of whom Browning wrote to Fanny Haworth at this time: 'a magnificent and poetical nature, who ... is in short "my literary father".' Fox, now separated from his wife, was living in his Bayswater house, somewhat unconventionally, with two of his children, his ward Eliza Flower and her sister Sarah and her husband. Browning asked Eliza to write settings for the songs in his next work, *Pippa Passes,* but her health was failing, and soon afterwards she died.

Then, there were new friends: one of them R. H. Horne, a man who had led an adventurous youth in Mexico before turning to literature, writing the epic *Orion*, befriending Elizabeth Barrett and giving *Sordello* its one appreciative review. Others were Joseph Arnould and Alfred Domett, both young barristers and minor poets, and like Browning members of the Camberwell 'Colloquials'. Arnould was to become a judge in Bombay, and in 1842 Domett left suddenly for New Zealand where he was to have a successful political career before returning to England just 30 years later, in 1872.

For twenty years he and Browning kept up their friendship by correspondence, and Domett is the 'Waring' of Browning's poem written soon after his disappearance:

> What's become of Waring
> Since he gave us all the slip,
> Chose land-travel or seafaring,
> Boots and chest or staff and scrip,
> Rather than pace up and down
> Any longer London town? ...
> Meantime, how much I loved him,
> I find out now I've lost him. ...

Then, having discovered what had become of Domett, and expecting him soon to return, Browning wrote: 'There you walk past our pond-rail (picking up one of the fallen horse-chestnuts), and now our gate-latch clicks, and now – ... 'Tis worth while running away to be so wished for again.'

But even more important than Domett's friendship was that of the generous John Kenyon, a portly, bald-headed man with a florid complexion and smiling blue eyes: 'the face of a Benedictine monk, and the joyous talk of a good fellow', according to Crabb Robinson. It turned out that he and Browning's father had been at school together, and as boys great friends, though they had not met since then. When Browning asked his father if he remembered a schoolfellow called John Kenyon, he replied by drawing a boy's face which his son recognised as the man of sixty. Interested in literature, Kenyon had himself published verse, and was now a wealthy man who encouraged and helped promising writers, including Elizabeth Barrett, who was a distant cousin. No wonder he became for the two young poets the 'dear Mr Kenyon' of their conversation and correspondence. Meanwhile Browning worked in his new room at New Cross, at the desk with the skull that housed his pet spider, or in the summer in the garden where spiders sat 'with arms akimbo' among the flowers and fruit trees, and soon had new work ready. When Edward Moxon published *Sordello*, it was with the advertisement that *Pippa Passes*, *King Victor and King Charles*, and *Mansoor the Hierophant*, the original name of *The Return of the Druses*, were almost ready, but after the failure of Sordello's story he was a little more chary about publishing further poems by Browning. However, as he was bringing out a cheap series of Elizabethan plays, he suggested that Browning's new work might be published in the same pamphlet form: 16 pages in double columns and bound in paper wrappers at a price of 6d. Browning agreed, and his father agreed to pay the cost, about £16 for each number; and so began the series of eight pamphlets under the general title of *Bells and Pomegranates*.

The recondite, though lovely, phrase was characteristic, one kind of obscurity which, on a much larger scale, had ruined *Sordello*, and it was only in the last pamphlet that, urged by Elizabeth Barrett, he explained:

... I only meant by that title to indicate an endeavour towards something like an alternation or mixture, of music with discoursing, sound with sense, poetry with thought; which looks too ambitious, thus expressed, so the symbol was preferred. It is little to the purpose, that such is actually one of the most familiar of the many Rabbinical (and Patristic) acceptations of the phrase; because I confess that, letting authority alone, I supposed the bare words, in such juxtaposition, would sufficiently convey the desired meaning. . . .

Bells-poetry, yes, but pomegranates-thought? And he did not add that the phrase comes from the little-known *Exodus* 28:

And beneath upon the hem of it thou shalt make pomegranates of blue, and of purple, and of scarlet, round about the hem thereof; and bells of gold between them round about:
A golden bell and a pomegranate, a golden bell and a pomegranate upon the hem of the robe round about.

The first of the series was published in April 1841: '*Pippa Passes*. By Robert Browning. Author of "Paracelsus" ' – not of 'Sordello'. There was a Preface, ending with a dedication to Serjeant Talfourd:

Two or three years ago I wrote a Play, about which the chief matter I much care to recollect at present is, that a Pit-full of good-natured people applauded it: – ever since I have been desirous of doing something in the same way that should better reward their attention. What follows I mean for the first of a series of Dramatical Pieces, to come out at intervals, and I amuse myself by fancying that the cheap mode in which they appear will for once help me to a sort of Pit-audience again. . . .

Pippa Passes had been advertised a year earlier as 'almost ready', but the failure of *Sordello*, and the main reason given by critics for its failure, its obscurity, probably made Browning spend some time in simplifying and clarifying its verse. In any event, it is very much easier to read than its predecessor, to understand without the irritation of having to pause and return to preceding lines to establish the sense. And the poems are, at first glance, very different: one the story of a young troubadour's life in the early thirteenth century, the other of a day in the life of a mill-girl in the mid-nineteenth century. Yet the themes are fundamentally the same – humanitarian; Sordello sacrifices himself for the people; Pippa *is* one of the people (or at least thinks she is, as did Sordello until the critical revelation of his birth), depicted by Browning as a victim of the early factory system, in danger of corruption by ruthless exploiters, but saved by her own courageous innocence. That Browning wrote, or rewrote, the conclusion of *Sordello* after his Italian visit and expedition to 'delicious Asolo' in 1838 is clear enough:

> Lo, on a heathy brown and nameless hill
> By sparkling Asolo, in mist and chill,
> Morning just up, higher and higher runs
> A child barefoot and rosy. See! the sun's
> On the square castle's inner-court's low wall ...
> Up and up goes he, singing all the while
> Some unintelligible words to beat
> The lark, God's poet. ...

The opening of *Pippa* is a development of the theme; the scene again Asolo, morning just up:

> Day!
> Faster and more fast,
> O'er night's brim, day boils at last:
> Boils, pure gold, o'er the cloud cup's brim. ...

And then Browning puts his description of morning by sparkling Asolo into his best-known, though not necessarily best, lyric:

> The year's at the spring
> And day's at the morn;
> Morning's at seven;
> The hill-side's dew-pearled;
> The lark's on the wing;
> The snail's on the thorn:
> God's in his heaven –
> All's right with the world.

The last two lines must not be taken too seriously, as they generally are, as a

51

summary of Browning's philosophy. He was an optimist, but here the lines are ironical. God might be in his heaven, but certainly all was not right with the world; Pippa might believe so, but it was Browning's purpose to show that it was not. For there is another theme underlying the humanitarian: that all our actions, all our speech, however trivial-seeming, influence the lives of others, for good or ill.

Thus, Pippa plans to spend her one day's annual holiday, trying to catch a glimpse of some of the fortunate, and therefore happy, people of Asolo and its neighbourhood. First, the villa where her employer lives, or rather lived, for he has just been murdered by his wife and her lover. Pippa's song, 'God's in his heaven,' makes them repent, and they prepare to die together. Pippa's passing has saved two souls, whatever that may mean, but killed two people.

In the second scene, 'Noon', the sculptor Jules has been tricked by a jealous rival into marrying an illiterate girl. When he finds what has happened he prepares to leave her, but Pippa's song, 'Give her but a least excuse to love me,' a legend of Queen Catherine, Lady of Asolo, makes him change his mind: not to kill the trickster, but to carry off his new love, his wife, to 'Some unsuspected isle in far-off seas'.

It is now evening, and the scene an old turret above Asolo. Evidently Browning had been reading Moxon's reprints of Elizabethan dramatists, at least Webster's *Duchess of Malfi*, with its melodramatic scene of the hollow and so dismal echo in the ruins of an ancient abbey: 'very deadly accent' – 'deadly accent', 'thing of sorrow' – 'thing of sorrow'. The weak-minded boy Luigi enters the turret with his mother, and addresses one of the withered wallflowers as the Emperor Franz, 'Come down and meet your fate!' And the echo – 'Meet your fate!' He is on his way to assassinate the Austrian Emperor, but his mother has almost dissuaded him when Pippa passes, singing 'Such grace had kings when the world begun.' 'Now that the world ends, 'tis God's voice calls,' Luigi cries, and watched by the secret police he rushes off to meet his fate in an attempt to kill the oppressor.

The last scene is at night in the cathedral palace. The Bishop slowly and smilingly reveals to his intendant that he knows him to be a murderer, but is about to agree to the temptation that his niece Felippa be got rid of by prostitution so that he may inherit his dead brother's estates, when he hears her innocent singing, and rises, shouting to his servants, 'Gag this villain! Remove him quick!' Whether his repentance will last till morning, whether he will tell Pippa that she is his niece and an heiress, we do not know, and she goes to bed wondering rather sadly,

Now, one thing I should like to really know:
How near I ever might approach all these
I only fancied being, this long day:
– Approach, I mean, so as to touch them, so
As to . . . in some way . . . move them – if you please,
Do good or evil to them some slight way.

'Good or evil.' Pippa is aware of the power of words, even when only over-heard, but she does not know that she has sent three people to their deaths, changed one man's indifference and hate into love, redeemed another, and saved herself from early death in a brothel.

Pippa is a landmark in Browning's career – he was not quite twenty-nine when it was published – his first really memorable major work. Although there were still a few awkward passages, the early obscurity had almost lifted, and it had become clear where his true genius lay – the dramatic poem or monologue. The characters are no longer Browning in disguise, but other people, men and women brought to life by his imaginative identification of self with them. It is this ability to assume the character of his creations, this sympathy, empathy, that makes him of all English poets the nearest to Chaucer and Shakespeare.

Then, it was in *Pippa* that Browning for the first time displayed the full range of his versatility, both as poet and technician. Not only is there blank verse and heroic couplets, but also more complex rhyme-schemes, from the opening description of daybreak to Pippa's lyrics and her last soliloquy; and, for the first time, prose: a sinister medium here, the language of panders, secret police, murderers and a worldly clergy, a language that anticipated by a hundred years the age of Hitler and the prose of Orwell. And even in the verse there is the beginning of a revolt against the smooth decorum of Victorian romanticism, a more colloquial realism: 'i' the dust o' the sill' – though this particular form was to become an idiosyncrasy.

Had *Sordello* been a triumph, critics would have applauded the appearance of *Pippa*, but it had failed, its successor was a shabby 6d pamphlet with the meaningless title 'Bells and Pomegranates. No. I', and such reviews as it had were, to say the least, unhelpful. All but one; in an unsigned article John Forster hailed it as 'without doubt, a piece of right inspiration. It is in a drama-tic form . . . but its highest beauty is lyrical.' But for others it was nearly as obscure as ever, the conundrums beginning with the very title-page. The *Spectator* found the moral tone offensive: wanton talk of paramours and 'common courtezans of the lowest class', a review that impelled Alfred Domett to write Peter Pindaresque verses 'On a Certain Critique on "Pippa Passes" (*Passes what ? – the critic's comprehension.*)'

53

> . . . A black squat beetle. . . .
> Has knocked himself full-butt, with blundering trouble,
> Against a mountain he can neither double
> Nor ever hope to scale. So like a free,
> Pert, self-conceited scarabaeus, he
> Takes it into his horny head to swear
> There's no such thing as any mountain there.

Pippa Passes was, or should have been, an admirable introduction to the 'Bells and Pomegranates' series, a new form of dramatic poem. But the young Browning wanted to write plays for the stage, and having found a friend in Macready understandably made the most of his opportunity. Even as early as the autumn of 1839, before *Sordello* was published, he had sent Macready his script of *King Victor and King Charles*; but the actor-manager would have nothing to do with it, and told Browning that it was 'a *great mistake*', giving reasons for his opinion and decision. Then, a year later, after the failure of *Sordello*, Browning submitted *The Return of the Druses*, and Macready wrote in his Diary: 'Read Browning's play, and with the deepest concern, I yield to the belief that he will *never write again* – to any purpose. I fear his intellect is not quite clear.' But Browning was not easily dismissed or discouraged, and a few days later, on 27 August 1840, Macready wrote: 'Browning came before I had finished my bath, and really *wearied* me with his obstinate faith in his poem of *Sordello*, and of his eventual celebrity, and also with his self-opinionated persuasions upon his *Return of the Druses*. I fear he is for ever gone.' Macready (and his audiences) wanted Character in Action, not Action in Character, so Browning set to work and before the end of the year was able to report: ' "The luck of the third adventure" is proverbial. I have written a spick and span new Tragedy (a sort of compromise between my own notion and yours – as I understand it, at least) and will send it to you if you care to be bothered so far. There is *action* in it, drabbing, stabbing, et autres gentillesses – who knows but the Gods may make me good even yet ?' The new tragedy was *A Blot in the 'Scutcheon*, but it was the autumn of 1841 before Macready read it, and December 1842 before he accepted it.

Pippa had been published in April 1841, and Browning had hoped to follow it in the spring of 1842 with his – successfully produced – new play, but Macready's long delay prevented this, and for 'Bells and Pomegranates II' he had to fall back, with some misgiving, on *King Victor and King Charles*, written three or four years earlier and rejected as unfit for the stage, 'a *great mistake*'. The only consolation was that the price was doubled: the *Pippa* pamphlet had been sixpence, *King Victor* was a shilling.

54

In his Preface Browning wrote that he hoped most readers would be acquainted with 'the chief circumstances of Victor's remarkable European career'. Such hopeful assumptions were a main reason for his early failure: that, for example, most educated people had read, as he had, the Life of Victor Amadeus in the *Biographie Universelle*, and knew that he was born in 1666, as a child succeeded his father as Duke of Savoy, married a niece of Louis XIV, against whose bullying he rebelled, sided with Austria from time to time, and in 1718 became first King of Sardinia. When his wife died he married his mistress, and in 1730 abdicated in favour of his son Charles. A year later he returned from his retirement and tried to resume the crown, but Charles confined him to prison where he died in 1732.

Browning takes up the story with the abdication of the autocratic, unscrupulous Victor, who has got himself into trouble both at home and abroad. He takes the title of Count, but 'The Count repents' says the cynical minister D'Ormea. Charles succeeds his father and, as champion of the people (like Sordello), gains their love as also the respect of foreign powers. Victor now returns to resume the crown, and Charles's devoted wife Polyxena accuses him:

> He thrust his child 'twixt danger and himself,
> And, when that child somehow stood danger out,
> Stole back with serpent wiles to ruin Charles.

'Do you repent, sir ?' D'Ormea adds. Charles himself puts the crown on his father's head, and Victor, at last realising the true stature of his son, dies with the words, 'You lied, D'Ormea! I do not repent.'

It is a fine theme, and the four characters are admirably portrayed; but again, the action is in the characters; we never see the characters in action. Nothing but words, Victor's central speech being nearly a hundred lines long. And again, the obscurity: 'What means he ?' Charles asks, as did Macready and the reviewers. 'Mr Browning allows his manner to come between his own fine conceptions and the public,' but there were those who hoped to see him soon 'take the one step more' out of the labyrinth in which he still lingered.

He took it later in the year, when Moxon suggested that 'Bells and Pomegranates III' should be a number of short poems instead of another unacted and unactable play. Towards the end of 1842, therefore, the third pamphlet of the series was published with the title *Dramatic Lyrics*, 'dramatic', as Browning emphasised in a prefatory note, for he still remembered Mill's analysis of *Pauline*:

Such Poems as the majority in this volume might also come properly enough,

55

I suppose, under the head of 'Dramatic Pieces'; being, though often Lyric in expression, always Dramatic in principle, and so many utterances of so many imaginary persons, not mine.

There were sixteen of these poems, and as in later collected editions they were to be distributed among different general titles it may be as well to give a list of them here:

> Cavalier Tunes. 1. Marching Along. 2. Give a Rouse. 3. Boot and Saddle.
> My Last Duchess.
> Count Gismond.
> Incident of the French Camp.
> Soliloquy of the Spanish Cloister.
> In a Gondola.
> Artemis Prologuises.
> Waring.
> Rudel to the Lady of Tripoli.
> Cristina.
> Johannes Agricola in Meditation.
> Porphyria's Lover.
> Through the Metidja to Abd-el-Kadr – 1842.
> The Pied Piper of Hamelin.

Most of these poems were recent, or fairly recent: 'Through the Metidja', for example, and 'Waring' must have been written after Domett sailed for New Zealand in the late spring of 1842; but two were at least seven years old: 'Johannes Agricola' and 'Porphyria's Lover' having appeared in Fox's *Monthly Repository* of January 1836.

The familiar obscurity was gone, or almost gone. It is true that the average reader could not be expected to know that Johannes Agricola was the sixteenth-century founder of Antinomianism, that Rudel was a twelfth-century trouba-dour writing to a princess in the symbolic language of his age, even that Cris-tina was an early nineteenth-century Queen of Spain. On the other hand, nothing could be clearer and simpler than the introductory songs of the Cava-liers and the Napoleonic 'Incident of the French Camp', while 'The Pied Piper' had just been written for Macready's little son to illustrate, and was included only at the last moment to fill the final pages of the pamphlet.

There can be few small books of verse that cover such a range of scene and subject: from Euripidean Greece to medieval France, from renaissance Italy and Germany to mid-nineteenth-century Algeria; from vengeance in Venice to murder for love, from brotherly hate in a Spanish cloister to the fun and pathos of a cheated medieval magician. And all these subjects demanded, and received, a different treatment, a different verse-form. There are the varying line-lengths, rhythms and rhyme-schemes of the dialogue, music and lyrics – 'The moth's kiss, first!' – of 'In a Gondola', the simple, sinister octosyllabics of 'Porphyria's Lover', the steady riding rhythm of 'Through the Metidja', the monotony of the desert journey emphasised by the single rhyme that runs through the forty lines (Browning wrote this in 1842 when, for his health, he was making daily rides on his uncle's horse), and there can have been very few Victorians who would have dared to begin – and end – a poem with

> Gr-r-r – there go, my heart's abhorrence!
> Water your damned flower-pots, do!. . . .
> *Ave Virgo !* Gr-r-r, you swine!

But the most dramatic, though scarcely lyrical, of the poems is 'My Last Duchess', which Browning wrote when he assumed the character of a sixteenth-century Duke of Ferrara. It is only 56 lines long, and the wonder is that the author of *Sordello* could pack within so small a compass material that might have been, but fortunately was not, expanded into a play for Macready. Browning had at last found the form that so exactly suited his genius; the dramatic monologue, in which the speaker reveals, brings to life, not only himself and the people about whom he talks, but also his audience. Thus, the thin-lipped Duke speaks in cold deliberate couplets to the agent of the Count whose daughter he proposes to marry, shows him the portrait of his last wife and, as a warning, describes her over-friendly manner and its end – death, or perhaps a convent:

>   I choose
> Never to stoop. Oh sir, she smiled no doubt,
> When'er I passed her; but who passed without
> Much the same smile ? This grew; I gave commands;
> Then all smiles stopped together. . . .
>   Nay, we'll go
> Together down, sir. Notice Neptune, though,
> Taming a sea-horse, thought a rarity,
> Which Claus of Innsbruck cast in bronze for me!

Not only is 'My Last Duchess' one of the finest things that Browning ever wrote, it was also something new in English poetry. Yet it passed unnoticed. John Forster admitted that there was much to object to in the *Dramatic Lyrics,*

57

though he found much more to praise, particularly the versification, but others complained of obscurity, lack of any dramatic quality in spite of the title, and wondered which were Bells, which Pomegranates.

When the poems were published in 1842 Macready was still hesitating about production of *A Blot in the 'Scutcheon*, so Browning decided that 'Bells and Pomegranates IV' should be the tragedy that he had rejected two years before, *The Return of the Druses*. The title was an unfortunate one: Bells – Pomegranates – Druses; Browning seemed to go out of his way to mystify his readers even before they began, for few of them could know that the Druses[5] were a Mohammedan sect with a secret religion based on belief in a God who from time to time revealed himself as man, Hakeem. Yet there was little obscurity either in matter or manner, in plot or verse, of the play published early in 1843.

The scene is a small island where a Druse colony is oppressed by the Prefect of the Knights-Hospitallers of neighbouring Rhodes. To free his people, Djabal professes to be Hakeem, planning to kill the Prefect and lead the Druses back to Lebanon. But it is the beautiful Anael who, to show her faith in Djabal, kills the Prefect. He confesses that he is not Hakeem, and she tells others, but when confronted with him she cries 'Hakeem!' and dies. Djabal stabs himself and, after walking a few steps towards Lebanon, calling, 'To the Mountain, Druses!' he falls dead.

Melodramatic, yes. But so is *Othello*. Which is not to compare Browning's tragedy with the splendour of Shakespeare's; Browning, it should be remembered, was only twenty-eight when he wrote. The first half is again action in character, not for Macready therefore, but then the tension quickens; for the first time we have character in action, and Djabal's last speech to Anael is true tragedy:

> And was it thou betrayedst me? 'Tis well!
> I have deserved this of thee, and submit.
> Nor 'tis much evil thou inflictest: life
> Ends here. The cedars shall not wave for us:
> For there was crime, and must be punishment. . . .

Yet it might almost be called 'The Tragedy of Loys', the virtuous – colourless – Breton Knight who discovers that his Prefect is a scoundrel, his friend Djabal an impostor, his love Anael a murderess. The scene of the Prefect's revelation of corruption to Loys, who is to succeed him, is in Browning's best vein of dramatic dialogue:

> ... Murcia, where my three fat manors lying,
> Purchased by gains here and the Nuncio's gold. ...

Then, when Loys threatens to unveil him, the Prefect asks blandly:

> To whom? – perhaps Sir Galeas, who in Chapter
> Shook his white head thrice – and some dozen times
> My hand next morning shook, for value paid!
> To that Italian saint, Sir Cosimo? –
> Indignant at my wringing year by year
> A thousand bezants from the coral-divers,
> As you recounted; felt the saint aggrieved?
> Well might he – I allowed for his half-share
> Merely one hundred. To Sir. ...

He retires behind the arras, for the first time for long years without feeling as though he lifted the lid of his tomb. Anael is waiting for him, and Loys hears 'The same hyena groan-like laughter' as she stabs him. The papal Nuncio speaks his valediction to the assembled Druses:

> While most he plotted for your good, that father
> (Alas, how kind, ye never knew) – lies slain.
> [*Aside*] (And hell's worm gnaw the glozing knave –)

The play – 'this "tragedy" (God wot!)' – passed almost unnoticed by the critics, and Macready missed a great opportunity in not accepting it for performance.

A few days before its publication in January 1843, Browning at last heard that Macready was prepared to produce *A Blot in the 'Scutcheon*. He had submitted this play of 'drabbing and stabbing' two years before, at the beginning of 1841; but that was the year in which Macready became manager of the Drury Lane theatre, and it was only when pressed by Forster at the end of September that he read it. He remembered *King Victor* and *The Druses*.

It is difficult to imagine how the fastidious author of these plays and *Dramatic Lyrics* could have descended so low. But then, he was an ambitious young man, desperately determined to gain a footing in the theatre despite, almost because of, former failure, and apparently prepared to succeed even if it meant pandering to the degraded taste of early-Victorian audiences. After all, his exact, and highly successful, contemporary Dickens had done much the same thing in his novels – *The Old Curiosity Shop* had just been published; but Dickens, in addition to being a genius in comedy, was a genuine sentimentalist, an irresistible combination, and Browning was not. Yet he seems never to have regretted writing the play.

59

The time is the eighteenth century, say 1740, the scene the country home of the feudal-minded Earl of Tresham, where he lives with his brother and sister-in-law, Austin and Guendolen, and his 14-year-old sister and ward, Mildred. His neighbour, the Earl of Mertoun, himself little more than a boy, calls to ask for Mildred's hand, to which Tresham readily agrees, before asking casually, 'Have you seen Lady Mildred, by the way?' Then hearing that a hooded man visits Mildred's room by night, he waylays him, finds him to be Mertoun, and mortally wounds him in a duel. Mildred dies of grief, and Tresham of poison.

Unlike the tragic tale of the star-crossed lovers Romeo and Juliet, it is a Victorian melodrama of a star-blessed couple with whom all should have gone well, and full of absurdities. If the young and highly eligible Mertoun loved Tresham's young sister, why did he seduce her instead of asking for her hand? Why had the earls of adjoining estates not met before? And why, after gaining Tresham's consent to marry Mildred, did Mertoun continue his nocturnal improprieties? Then, what girl could fall for a lover who sang 'There's a woman like a dew-drop,' and compared her voice to 'the well's bubbling, the bird's warble'? Perhaps the silly girl who says, not once, but three times, 'I was so young – I had no mother.' Her brother is as mawkish as she is sentimental, and talks to the dear and ancient yew trees that his fathers planted about the blot in his 'scutcheon. Guendolen is the only credible character: masterful, she tells her husband what to do; intuitive, she guesses Mildred's secret; and if only she had been given a few more minutes would have made all well.

This was the play that Macready read, thought just possible for performance, but remembering his former doubts about Browning as dramatist – 'I fear he is for ever gone' – hesitated to accept, so Forster sent the script to his friend Dickens for his opinion. But 1842 was the year of Dickens's visit to America, a lengthy business in those days, and it was the end of November before he replied. Forster must have known that he would approve, but could scarcely have expected this:

Browning's play has thrown me into a perfect passion of sorrow. To say there is anything in its subject save what is lovely, true, deeply affecting, full of the best emotion, the most earnest feeling, and the most true and tender source of interest, is to say that there is no light in the sun, and no heat in the blood. It is full of genius, natural and great thoughts, profound and yet simple and beautiful in its vigour. I know of nothing that is so affecting, nothing in any books I have ever read, as Mildred's recurrence to that 'I was so young – I had no mother.' I know of no love like it, no passion like it. And I swear it is a tragedy that *must* be played; and must be played, moreover, by Macready. There are some things I would have changed if I could. . . . But the tragedy I never shall forget, or less vividly remember than I do now. And if you tell Browning that I have seen it, tell him that I believe from my soul there is no man living (and not many dead) who could produce such a work.

In spite of this eulogy and assurance that the tragedy *must* be played, played by Macready, it was not without misgiving that, towards the end of January 1843, he agreed to produce the play.

He was right to question the wisdom of his decision. He was unwell, over-worked, worried by domestic and financial troubles; and Browning was impatient. He recorded the fortnight's progress, if that is the right word, in his Diary. On Saturday the 28th the prompter read the play to the cast, some of whom, as he told Browning the next day, thought it very funny. On Tuesday, feeling very unwell, he found Browning waiting for him at the theatre, very angry that the doorkeeper had not treated him with more courtesy: 'I fear he is a very conceited man.' The next day he told him that he was too busy to take part, and that Samuel Phelps would play Tresham. Then, on February 6th, Phelps being too ill to rehearse, he decided to understudy the part, and by the 9th, two days before the first performance, he had resolved to play Tresham after all.

February 10th. Began the consideration and study of the part of Tresham, which was to occupy my single thoughts till accomplished. About a quarter past one a note came, informing me that Mr Phelps would do the part, if he 'died for it,' so that my time had been lost. Arrived, I applied to business; offered to give to Browning and Mr Phelps the benefit of my consideration and study in the cuts, etc. I had made one I thought particularly valuable, not letting Tresham die, but consigning him to a convent. Browning, however, in the worst taste, manner, and spirit, declined any further alterations, expressing himself perfectly satisfied with the manner in which Mr Phelps executed Lord Tresham. I had no more to say. I could only think Mr Browning a very disagreeable and offensively mannered person. *Voilà tout!*

February 11th. Directed the rehearsal of *Blot on the 'Scutcheon,* and made many valuable improvements. Browning seemed desirous to explain or qualify the strange carriage and temper of yesterday, and laid much blame on Forster for irritating him.

Saw the play of *Blot on the 'Scutcheon,* which was badly acted in Phelp's and Mrs Stirling's [Guendolen] parts – pretty well in Anderson's [Mertoun], very well in Helen Faucit's [Mildred]. I was *angry* after the play about the call being directed without me.

Browning wrote his version of the affair in a letter forty years later. The actors had laughed at his tragedy because it had been read to them by the prompter, 'a grotesque person with a red nose and wooden leg, ill at ease in the love scenes.' And when he insisted that it was only fair that Phelps should keep the part that had been given him, 'Macready at once wished to reduce the importance of the "play" – as he styled it in the bills, – tried to leave out so much of the text, that I baffled him by getting it printed in four-and-twenty hours, by Moxon's assistance.' And not a shilling, Browning wrote, was spent on new scenery and costume.

Mrs Orr, in her *Life of Browning*, added a footnote, for she well remembered his telling her how, when he supported Phelps, 'he drove his hat more firmly on to his head, and said to Macready, "I beg pardon, sir, but you have given the part to Mr Phelps, and I am satisfied that he should act it;" and how Macready, on hearing this, crushed up the MS, and flung it on to the ground. He [Browning] also admitted that his own manner had been provocative; but he was indignant at what he deemed the unjust treatment which Mr Phelps had received.'

After its performance, Forster did his best for the play: 'a work of so much rare beauty, and of such decisive originality.' But other critics were not quite so sure: 'a very puzzling and unpleasant piece of business. ... A few of the audience laughed, others were shocked, and many applauded.' 'Aversion is the predominant feeling created. This was audibly, though not loudly expressed, on two or three occasions during the first representation; but it took a ludicrous turn towards the close, and the catastrophe elicited an involuntary titter.'

In brief, the play was a failure, and ran for only three nights. But it was partly Browning's own fault, as Forster told him. To put on a play at Macready's theatre without Macready in the lead was suicidal, and the touchy, humourless actor had, of course, expected the author to implore him to retain the part of Tresham. But, oddly enough, Forster did not show Browning Dickens's letter, which he read for the first time thirty years later in Forster's *Life of Dickens*. Their friendship was wearing thin. And with Macready Browning was no longer on speaking terms. They saw one another occasionally at other people's houses: in 1846, for example, when 'Browning did not speak to me, the *puppy*.' But reconciliation followed a few years later when Browning, happily married and living in Italy, heard of Mrs Macready's death and wrote to his old friend, recalling the happy days of intimacy with him and his family.

A Blot in the 'Scutcheon was published on the day of its first performance, 11 February 1843, as 'Bells and Pomegranates V', and fortunately for

4. Edmund Kean as Richard III, a performance that inspired
Browning to become a dramatist. *The Raymond Mander & Joe
Mitchenson Theatre Collection.*

5. 'The author of Paracelsus' in 1837: 'just a trifle of a dandy.'
A sketch by Comte Amédée de Ripart Monclar.
Courtesy Armstrong Browning Library, Baylor University.

BELLS AND POMEGRANATES.

Nº· I.—PIPPA PASSES.

BY ROBERT BROWNING,

AUTHOR OF "PARACELSUS."

ADVERTISEMENT.

Two or three years ago I wrote a Play, about which the chief matter I much care to recollect at present is, that a Pit-full of goodnatured people applauded it :—ever since, I have been desirous of doing something in the same way that should better reward their attention. What follows I mean for the first of a series of Dramatical Pieces, to come out at intervals, and I amuse myself by fancying that the cheap mode in which they appear will for once help me to a sort of Pit-audience again. Of course such a work must go on no longer than it is liked; and to provide against a certain and but too possible contingency, let me hasten to say now—what, if I were sure of success, I would try to say circumstantially enough at the close—that I dedicate my best intentions most admiringly to the Author of "Ion"—most affectionately to Serjeant Talfourd.

LONDON:
EDWARD MOXON, DOVER STREET.
MDCCCXLI.

6. The beginning of recovery after the disaster of *Sordello* (1840). In the original pamphlet the Advertisement appeared on p. 2: it has been inserted here on the title page.
Victoria & Albert Museum.

7. 'Which is the poison to poison her, prithee?' *The Laboratory.*
Watercolour by D. G. Rossetti. *Reproduced by permission of
Birmingham Museum and Art Gallery*

Browning, now that he had broken with Macready, a rival star had recently risen in the world of the theatre: Edmund Kean's son, Charles, a young man of Browning's age, who had just married the actress Ellen Tree. Kean now offered Browning 'two or three hundred pounds' if he would write a play for him and his wife, and in March 1844 he read it to them. They liked it, as well they might, for it was just the play for a newly-married couple to perform, almost a wedding-masque, but Kean wanted to postpone production for a year, during which time it was to remain unpublished. Browning, however, refused; Kean could retain the right to perform, but meanwhile it would be published. He must keep his name before his readers, he said, and could not risk losing the good fortune that appeared to be approaching. On the day that he read his play to the Keans he sent it to Moxon, and a month later it appeared as 'Bells and Pomegranates VI. Colombe's Birthday.' It was dedicated, appropriately enough, to 'Barry Cornwall', pseudonym of Bryan Waller Proctor, who had recently written a *Life of Edmund Kean.*

Colombe's Birthday is little more than a delightful fairy-tale of the seventeenth-century. On her birthday Colombe, who has been Duchess of Juliers and Cleves for exactly a year, learns that her cousin Prince Berthold is the rightful heir to the duchies. He offers her marriage, but a young advocate, Valence, has just arrived in Juliers to plead the cause of the poor and oppressed in Cleves. She falls in love with this honest, humane young man and, finally, renouncing the duchies, into his arms. To add to the fairy-tale atmosphere, the action takes place in the course of one day, or rather, half a day, for it is noon before Colombe meets Valence, less than twelve hours before confessing her love. As a contrast to this innocent romance, there is a background of intrigue, of self-seeking courtiers, the people's oppressors who are prepared to shift their allegiance from Colombe to Berthold:

> Well 'tis my comfort, you could never call me
> The People's Friend! The People keep their word –
> I keep my place. . . .
> Now see: we tax and tithe them, pill and poll,
> They wince and fret enough, but pay they must
> – We manage that. . . .

But those are the morning words of Guibert, who repents by night and prepares to serve Colombe in her remaining castle of Ravestein, for "Tis my Birthday, too!'

When published, *Colombe's Birthday* attracted little attention. There was praise for its chivalrous spirit and comparative clarity of expression, but

63

Forster, while admitting that the play was further proof of Browning's genius, concluded enigmatically, 'As far as he has gone, we abominate his tastes as much as we respect his genius.' Another friendship was broken, at least for a time; and perhaps Forster's review was the reason why Charles Kean did not accept the play. However, it had a short though successful run when produced in 1853 by Helen Faucit, the heroine of *Strafford* and *A Blot in the 'Scutcheon*.

Between March 1842 and March 1844 Browning had published – at his father's expense – four plays, only one of which had been performed, and even that was a failure that had cost him the friendship of Macready. And now *Colombe's Birthday* had been declined by Kean and led to estrangement from Forster. His innate optimism flagged, he felt himself a failure, and the headaches to which he had always been subject grew worse and more frequent. Although he had another short play, *A Souls Tragedy*, in his desk, he knew that it would not be acted, and did not feel inclined to add it to the 'Bells and Pomegranates' series; so, although he did not care for publishing single poems in periodicals, he sent a few to *Hood's Magazine* in the summer of 1844. Thus, 'The Laboratory' appeared in the June number: a Websterian melodrama-in-little, a dramatic monologue within the forty-eight lines of which the speaker reveals not only herself, but also her former lover and his new love, her victim, and the old poison-maker himself:

> What a drop! She's not little, no minion like me!
> That's why she ensnared him: this never will free
> The soul from those masculine eyes, – say, 'no!'
> To that pulse's magnificent come-and-go.

Very different were the 'Garden Fancies' of the July number, two poems inspired by the Browning garden at New Cross: the first with the memorable lines to the flower with

> Its soft meandering Spanish name. . . .
> I must learn Spanish, one of these days,
> Only for that slow sweet name's sake.

Elizabeth Barrett was to write of 'that beautiful and musical use of the word "meandering", which I never remember having seen used in relation to *sound* before.' She might also have remarked on the sound of the last line: the slow music of its long chiming vowels and final five stressed monosyllables. Different again was the humorous 'Sibrandus Schafnaburgensis', the pedant whose book Browning dropped into a damp crevice in the garden, then

went in-doors, brought out a loaf
Half a cheese, and a bottle of Chablis;
Lay on the grass and forgot the oaf
Over a jolly chapter of Rabelais.

Rabelais, as one might guess, was an old favourite of Browning's.

Yet he was tired – 'my *head* sings and whirls', he wrote to Domett – and he decided to take a holiday. (It would also be a holiday – at home – for his amanuensis, his devoted sister Sarianna.) In August, therefore, he sailed again for Italy. Off Cape Trafalgar he wrote 'Here's to Nelson's memory!', then shortly afterwards 'Nobly, nobly Cape Saint Vincent to the North-west died away,' and off the African coast another, though less obviously appropriate home thought from abroad, 'How They Brought the Good News from Ghent to Aix.' He had been long enough at sea, he wrote later, 'to appreciate even the fancy of a gallop on a certain good horse "York", then in my stable at home.'

His first Italian visit in 1838 had been to the northern plain of Lombardy in search of the scenes of *Sordello*, but now, in September 1844, he landed at Naples, where a small band of patriots had just been executed for leading a revolt against Bourbon rule. He visited the scene where Shelley had written his 'Stanzas in Dejection', and made friends with a young Italian who accompanied him on his first visit to Rome. There he seems to have been more interested in Renaissance than Imperial remains, and the church of Santa Prassede, restored in the fifteenth century, was to inspire the writing of 'The Bishop Orders his Tomb.' Travelling north to Leghorn, he called on the last man to have seen Shelley alive, Edward Trelawny, then suffering stoically from an old bullet-wound. He paid his first visit to Florence, treasure-town of Renaissance art – and so much more – and so once again across the Alps, down the Rhine and back to London, which he reached in December, physically tired no doubt, but mentally refreshed.

4. Elizabeth Barrett
1845–46

AMONG the new books to be read when Browning returned to New Cross after his four months' visit to Italy were the two volumes of Elizabeth Barrett's *Poems*. He had read and admired her previous book, *The Seraphim*, but here was something that touched him more nearly, for in the middle of the long 'Lady Geraldine's Courtship' came the verse:

Or at times a modern volume, – Wordsworth's solemn-thoughted idyl,
Howitt's ballad-verse, or Tennyson's enchanted reverie, –
Or from Browning some 'Pomegranate', which, if cut deep down the middle,
Shows a heart within blood-tinctured, of a veined humanity!

At this time, 1844, Elizabeth Barrett was 38, six years older than Browning. The eldest child of Edward Barrett, a wealthy owner of slave plantations in Jamaica, she was born at Coxhoe Hall in Durham, but three years later the family moved south to another country house, Hope End, which her father built in Hertfordshire, 'a Turkish house ... crowded with minarets and domes,' as Elizabeth was to describe it, and there she, her two sisters and eight brothers spent their childhood and youth. She was a precocious child, and when only twelve wrote an epic in four books, 'The Battle of Marathon', which was privately printed at her father's expense, and her reading of Pope's translation of Homer inspired her to study Greek and Latin – unladylike pursuits in those days. *An Essay on Mind, with other Poems* was published anonymously in 1826, shortly before her mother's death, and a translation of *Prometheus Bound* in 1833. This was the year of abolition of slavery within the British Empire, and the now not-quite-so-wealthy Mr Barrett sold his country house and moved to Sidmouth on the coast of Devon, before settling in London, finally, in 1838, at 50 Wimpole Street.

The Seraphim was published at about this time, and Elizabeth now made the acquaintance of a number of people whom Browning had met after the success of *Paracelsus* in 1835. There was Hengist Horne, with whom she kept up a long correspondence and collaborated in his *New Spirit of the Age*. Landor she met,

66

and Wordsworth, solemn and calm, and Miss Mitford who became a great friend. But most important of all was her old friend and cousin John Kenyon, a man of substance in every sense of the word, who was to play the part of fairy-godfather to herself and her future husband.

The year 1838 was a critical one for Elizabeth. As a girl she had suffered from acute pains in the head and back, which, however, had been eased by opium and her healthy life in the country. But the smoky atmosphere of London brought on again the former symptoms, perhaps of consumption, the triumphant Victorian disease of Browning's adolescent 'Dance of Death'. She was, therefore, sent again to the Devonshire coast, to stay with an aunt in Torquay, where her family took it in turns to look after her. While there she wrote, 'There are so many mercies close around me that God's being seems proved to me, *demonstrated* to me, by His manifested love.' She was a very religious woman, a mystical Nonconformist, but her faith was almost shaken when 'Bro', her eldest and adored brother Edward, was drowned while staying with her. She felt responsible, for she had asked him to prolong his visit, and for months, as she told Miss Mitford, she could not read, could understand little that was said to her. She longed to escape from the scene of the tragedy, but it was the autumn of 1841 before she was fit to travel back to Wimpole Street. There, following doctors' orders, she was confined to a dim and airless room to which her father would come every night to pray beside her. It was a situation that he must have appreciated, this patriarchal, tyrannic Victorian father of eleven children, terrified of sex and determined to prevent any of them marrying. Elizabeth, at least, was safe, submissive – and loving. As she was to write to Browning: 'But what you do *not* see, what you *cannot* see, is the deep tender affection behind and below all those patriarchal ideas of governing grown up children "in the way they *must* go!" and there never was (under the strata) a truer affection in a father's heart. . . . The evil is in the system – and he simply takes it to be his duty to rule, and to make happy according to his own views of the propriety of happiness. . . . But he loves us through and through it – and *I*, for one, love *him*!'

That was written in August 1845, but at the beginning of January Browning had read Elizabeth's Dedication of her *Poems* with 'tenderest and holiest affection' to her father. However, he was more interested in the poet than in the father, and when Mr Kenyon heard of his admiration he begged him to write to his invalid cousin, for 'great souls jump at sympathy.' So, on January 10th Browning wrote from New Cross: 'I love your verses with all my heart, dear Miss Barrett . . . this great living poetry of yours . . . the fresh strange music, the affluent language, the exquisite pathos, and true new brave thought. . . . I do, as I say, love these books with all my heart, and I love you too.'[6] An unconventional self-introduction to a lady whom 'Yours ever faithfully Robert Browning' had never met.

Next day his 'obliged and faithful Elizabeth B. Barrett' replied from 50 Wimpole Street: 'I thank you, dear Mr Browning, from the bottom of my heart . . . Sympathy is dear – very dear to me: but the sympathy of a poet, and of such a poet, is the quintessence of sympathy to me! . . . Winters shut me up as they do dormouse's eyes; in the spring, *we shall see*: and I am so much better that I seem turning round to the outward world again. . . . Mr Kenyon often speaks of you – dear Mr Kenyon! . . .'

So began the correspondence, the almost daily shuttle of letters between New Cross and Wimpole Street, that was to last nearly two years: a correspondence that Browning himself might have conceived as a five-part romance, part one being the four months leading up to his first meeting with Elizabeth. We are introduced to some of their friends and aquaintances: thus, Elizabeth writes of dear Mr Kenyon, of course, and dear Miss Mitford, who was the first to tell her about the grand scene in *Pippa Passes*, and poor Hengist Horne whose *New Spirit of the Age* (to which she had contributed essays) had been so infamously treated by his vicious and jealous contemporaries. Browning mentions Tennyson, who 'reads the *Quarterly* and does as they bid him. . . . Oh me!' and Carlyle of the grand head, whom he knows so well and so loves and John Mill, who wrote a marginal note in 'the little book I first printed when a boy.'

Elizabeth, most courageous of women, with a delightful sense of humour, tells Browning something about herself: how she is what her Italian tutor used to call *testa lunga*, headlong, and that headlong she remains, expecting the thunder to be as quick as the lightning; and, not altogether humorously perhaps, how she heard of the skull and spider on Browning's desk from Browning himself, for 'are you not aware that these are the days of mesmerism and clairvoyance? Are you an infidel?' Then, 'I grew up in the country – had no social opportunities, had my heart in books and poetry, and my experience in reveries. . . . I seem to live while I write – it is life, for me.' She has more to say about Browning and his work than about her own, much of it acute criticism. He is, she tells him, both subjective (Browning must have winced) and objective in the habits of his mind, and can deal 'both with abstract thought and with human passion in the most passionate sense.' Yet, 'a great dramatic power may develop itself otherwise than in the formal drama,' and she hopes that he will write a poem unassociated with the stage. 'I reverence the drama, but – ' She returns to the theme a month later: 'And what is "Luria"? A poem and not a drama? I mean, a poem not in the dramatic form? Well! I have wondered at you sometimes, not for daring, but for bearing to trust your noble works into the great mill of the "rank, popular" playhouse, to be ground to pieces between the teeth of vulgar actors and actresses. I, for one, would as soon have "my soul among lions".'

This was in reply to Browning's brief mention of 'this darling "Luria" – so safe in my head, and a tiny slip of paper I cover with my thumb!' He took note of what Elizabeth had said, and in his reply wrote apologetically: 'That "Luria" you enquire about, shall be my last play – for it is but a play, woe's me! I have one done here, "A Soul's Tragedy", as it is properly enough called, but *that* would not do to end with (and end I will).' He could afford to do so, or rather, he could not afford not to do so; as a dramatist, a writer for the theatre, he was a failure, and for some time had had other things in mind. He had already told Elizabeth that 'You speak out, *you*, – I only make men and women speak – give you truth broken into prismatic hues, and fear the pure white light, even if it is in me, but I am going to try.' It was not quite true – fortunately. 'A great dramatic power may develop itself otherwise than in the formal drama,' she had written; 'I only make men and women speak,' he wrote. *Only!* Like Shakespeare, for example? But if he lacked Shakespeare's genius for the stage, he could emulate Chaucer, modify his form and develop his technique, make men and women speak and reveal themselves in poems of any length, from a dozen lines to a dozen books. For it was men and women, their characters and motives, that so passionately interested him, and his new work was to be such dramatic romances as 'The Flight of the Duchess' and 'a certain "Saul" ' to which he made tantalising reference. Yet he confessed that, unlike Elizabeth, he took no pleasure in writing, in the mere act, the sort of pleasure that painting, for example, would give him. He did not even care for reading now, but preferred the world itself and pictures of it to writings about it. As for society, he had 'always hated it' and had put up with it for the last six or seven years only for fear of letting slip some golden opportunity. Yet, on 12 May, after a silence of ten days, he wrote, 'I have gone out a great deal of late, and my head took to ringing such a literal alarum' that he had cancelled all engagements. 'I thought I never could be unwell,' he had written on 3 May, but for the last two months he had suffered from a constant pain in the head.

His own health, however, was unimportant in comparison with that of Elizabeth, and he implored her *always* to enclose a little bulletin in her letters.

On 5 March she was *'essentially better'*, by the 20th she had not been very well, but a month later was recovering 'from the prostration of the severe cold'. Then on 6 May comes the first ominous reference to opium, the drug long ago recommended by her doctors: 'I think better of sleep than I ever did, now that she will not easily come near me except in a red hood of poppies.' However, she concluded, 'I am certainly stronger and better than I was .. and I *shall* be better still.' Browning's solicitude was not altogether disinterested, for on her health depended his first meeting her. Thus in February he wrote with breezy encouragement, 'Real warm Spring, dear Miss Barrett, . . . and in Spring I shall see you, surely see you.' In March he asked, 'Do you think I shall see you in two months, three months ?' April was cold, 'the bad wind back again,' Elizabeth prostrated, but on 13 May he asked simply, 'Do see me when you can.' Unfortunately that was in the letter complaining about the singing in his head, and Elizabeth replied mischievously that he must keep quiet until it had gone, though later she relented and told him that he could now come any afternoon between two and six. 'I will call at 2 on Tuesday,' he wrote; and she again, 'Let it be three instead of two.' She was nervous, anxious to meet him, but understandably reluctant to let him see her faded beauty. Eight years earlier, before her illness had confined her to an airless and dusty room, she was, wrote Miss Mitford, 'a slight girlish figure, very delicate, with exquisite hands and feet, a round face, with a most noble forehead, a large mouth, beautifully formed, and full of expression, lips like parted coral, . . . large dark eyes, with such eyelashes, resting on the cheek when cast down; when turned upward, touching the flexible and expressive eyebrow; a dark complexion, with cheeks literally as bright as the dark china rose; a profusion of silky, dark curls, and a look of youth and modesty hardly to be expressed.' But now her youth's proud livery was tattered, and the former beauty whom Browning met in her Wimpole Street room on the afternoon of Tuesday 20 May 1845 was a worn and pallid woman of thirty-nine who looked more than her years.

On his return to New Cross he wrote to ask how she was after his visit, hoping that he had done nothing to offend or upset her, that he had not talked too loudly or stayed too long. Next morning she assured him that there had been nothing wrong, but everything right, and asked him to come on the following Tuesday, 'and again, when you like.' On the same day Browning wrote another letter, but it was Friday evening before she replied – to his reckless and passionate declaration of love. She was flattered and flustered. He was a handsome, brilliant, active young man – just thirty-three – with the world before him; she was six years older, a prematurely aged woman confined to a sofa in a sick-room by a devoted father who forbade his children to marry. How could she possibly marry Robert Browning, and perhaps ruin his career? Yet, she loved him, or at least, could not bear to lose him as a friend. So she wrote:

I intended to write to you last night and this morning, and could not, – you do not know what pain you give me in speaking so wildly. And if I disobey you, my dear friend, in speaking, (I for my part) of your wild speaking, I do it, not to displease you, but to be in my own eyes, and before God, a little more worthy, or less unworthy, of a generosity from which I recoil by instinct and at the first glance, yet conclusively. . . .

Listen to me then in this. You have said some intemperate things – fancies – which you will not say over again, nor unsay, but *forget at once*, and *for ever*, *having said at all* . . . And this you will do *for my sake* who am your friend (and you have none truer) – and this I ask because it is a condition necessary to our future liberty of intercourse. You remember – surely you do – that I am in the most exceptional of positions. . . .

Now, if there should be one word of answer attempted to this; or of reference; *I must not – I will not see you again* – and you will justify me later in your heart. So for my sake you will not say it – I think you will not – and spare me the sadness of having to break through an intercourse just as it is promising pleasure to me; to me who have so many sadnesses and so few pleasures. . . .

You are not displeased with me? *no, that* would be hail and lightning together. . . . And if I have said one word to vex you, pity me for having had to say it – and for the rest, may God bless you far beyond the reach of vexation from my words or my deeds!

Your friend in grateful regard,
E.B.B.

When Browning received that letter on the Saturday morning, he replied lengthily, and not very coherently, by return:

Don't you remember I told you, once on a time, that you 'knew nothing of me'? whereat you demurred – but I meant what I said, and knew it was so. To be grand in a simile, for every poor speck of a Vesuvius or a Stromboli in my microcosm there are huge layers of ice and pits of black cold water – and I make the most of my two or three fire-eyes, because I know by experience, alas, how these tend to extinction – and the ice grows and grows – still this last is true part of me, most characteristic part, *best* part perhaps, and I disown nothing – only, – when you talked of '*knowing* me'! Still, I am utterly unused, of these late years particularly, to dream of communicating anything about *that* to another person (all my writings are purely dramatic as I am always anxious to say) that when I make never so little an attempt, no wonder if I *bungle* notably. . . .

Will you not think me very brutal if I tell you I could almost smile at your misapprehension of what I meant to write? – Yet I *will* tell you, because it will undo the bad effect of my thoughtlessness, and at the same time exemplify the point I have all along been honestly earnest to set you right upon – my real inferiority to you; just that and no more. I wrote to you, in an unwise moment, on the spur of being again 'thanked', and, unwisely writing just as if thinking to myself, said what must have looked absurd enough as seen apart from the horrible counterbalancing never-to-be-written *rest of me* – by the side of which, could it be written and put before you, my note would sink to its proper and relative place, and become a mere 'thank you' for your good opinion. ...

Will you forgive me, on promise to remember for the future, and be more considerate? ... I am, from my heart, sorry that by a foolish fit of inconsideration I should have given pain for a minute to you. ... I shall be too much punished if, for this piece of mere inconsideration, you deprive me, more or less, or sooner or later, of the pleasure of seeing you, – a little over-boisterous gratitude for which, perhaps, caused all the mischief! ...

Pray write me a line to say, 'Oh – if *that's* all!' and remember me for good (which is very compatible with a moment's stupidity) and let me not for one fault, (and that the only one that shall be), lose any *pleasure* – for your friendship I am sure I have not lost – God bless you, my dear friend!

R. Browning.

The next day, Sunday, Elizabeth wrote to apologise humbly for having treated so simple a matter so solemnly, but defended herself with another piece of acute criticism: 'I have observed before in my own mind, that a good deal of what is called obscurity in you, arises from a habit of very subtle association; so subtle, that you are probably unconscious of it, and the effect of which is to throw together on the same level and in the same light, things of likeness and unlikeness – till the reader grows confused as I did, and takes one for another.' And now they were to forget all about this exquisite nonsense, never again to mention it, but shuffle the cards and begin the game again, and he was to come on Wednesday at 3 o'clock. Finally, she returned the offending letter, as he had asked, and advised him to burn it, which he did.

So ended the brief and violent second scene of their romance. The surprise and surprising assault had failed, and Browning prepared for a long siege, which was to begin with 'enter R.B. – next Wednesday.'

> To-morrow we meet the same then, dearest?
> May I take your hand in mine?
> Mere friends are we, – well, friends the merest
> Keep much that I resign: ....
>
> Yet I will but say what mere friends say,
> Or only a thought stronger;
> I will hold your hand but as long as all may,
> Or so very little longer.

All Browning's writings were not as purely dramatic as he would have had Elizabeth believe: certainly not 'The Lost Mistress.'

So the game began again, though, as might be expected, less formally. They were no longer 'Yours faithfully Robert Browning' and 'Elizabeth B. Barrett', but 'R.B.' and 'E.B.B.' And there were anecdotes: how poor old Wordsworth, in a borrowed bag-wig and a superfluity of etiquette, fell upon both knees when receiving the Laureateship from the Queen; about Flush, the spaniel that Miss Mitford had given Elizabeth; about Miss Martineau and mesmerism; and Elizabeth wrote a vivid description of a thunderstorm in her youth – she was frightened of thunderstorms – and of her present life in Wimpole Street, like Mariana in the moated grange: 'my father is out all day and my brothers and sisters are in and out, and with too large a public of noisy friends for me to bear;' and as Browning was 'opined to talk generally in blank verse' they avoided her room when he was there. Even dear Mr Kenyon was sometimes almost a nuisance when he proposed calling at a time that had been reserved for Browning's weekly visit. And there was his sister Sarianna as well as Browning himself to be thanked for flowers from their New Cross garden.

He, in turn, assured Elizabeth that he loved to have few friends and to live alone, dressed, as when he wrote, in a blue shirt instead of formal gentlemanly clothes. One friendship, however, was renewed when John Forster called in October, or rather, its repair began, 'as the snail repairs its battered shell.'

Elizabeth must have been one of the most modest of remarkable women. There can be few who would have written to a lover: 'I have one advantage over you, one, of which women are not fond of boasting – that of being *older by years*.' And again: 'To judge at all of a work of yours, I must *look up to it*, and *far up* – because whatever faculty *I* have is included in your faculty, and with a great rim all round it besides!' 'I am not servile,' she added, 'but sincere, meaning what I say.' And she told Browning what she thought of the poems that he was preparing for publication and sent her to read. She loved them: 'if people do not cry out about these poems, what are we to think of the world?' Yet he did sometimes make things unnecessarily difficult for his readers; could he not 'stoop to the vulgarism' of giving his shorter pieces the clue of a title? The fragment of 'Saul' was exquisite, and she besought him to finish it, but best of all she liked the romantic 'Flight of the Duchess', its rhymes 'all clashing together as by natural attraction'. Browning, in his turn, humbly accepted all her suggestions for improvement.

Elizabeth constantly asked about his health, the pain in his head, but he lightly assured her that that was improving, and his great concern was for her.

73

He encouraged her to walk about her room, to go downstairs, to drive in the Park, until she was able to report that she walked upright every day. That was in October, but as early as July her aunt had been trying to persuade her father to send her to Malta or Alexandria for the winter. At the beginning of September her doctor recommended Pisa, and Browning wrote: 'if one could transport you quietly to Pisa, save you all worry, – what might one not expect!' 'Oh, to be in Pisa!' He too would be there. On the 17th, however, Elizabeth reported that it was all over with Pisa, and on the 25th that it seemed best to go to Malta – 'without excluding Pisa'. So plans went half-heartedly ahead – '*Don't* think too hardly of poor Papa' – until she wrote on 14 October: 'do not think it my fault – but *I do not go to Italy* – it has ended as I feared. What passed between George and Papa there is no need of telling; only the latter said that I "might go if I pleased but that going it would be under his heaviest displeasure".' She was quite prepared to incur that displeasure, but not to bring it on her brother and sister; she would risk another London winter, but 'the bitterest fact of all is, that I had believed Papa to have loved me more than he obviously does.' Browning was infuriated by the oriental tyranny of the man he had never met, but wrote reassuringly: 'Be sure, my own, dearest love, that this is for the best.'

'My own, dearest love.' Browning's siege tactics had progressed in the course of the last few months. In July Elizabeth had been 'my dear, first and best friend; my friend!' But a change came at the end of August when she told him the full story of Bro's drowning at Torquay; how, when she had asked if he might stay with her longer, her father had replied that he did not refuse his consent, but that it was '*very wrong in me to exact such a thing.*' In his reply Browning wrote, 'Let me say now – *this only once* – that I loved you from my soul, and gave you my life,' loved, that is, as soon as he saw her. This time she did not reprove but, thinking always of him, 'Your life! if you gave it to me and I put my whole heart into it; what should I put but anxiety, and more sadness than you were born to? . . . Therefore we must leave this subject.' Another repulse, but at least, thanks to her brother George, he had learned her pet name and wrote it triumphantly – 'Ba'. He had also learned, for she had told him, that she was financially independent of her father, with an income of three or four hundred a year, and a fortnight later he wrote: 'When I first met you . . . I supposed you to labour under an incurable complaint – and, of course, to be completely dependent on your father. . . . Now again the circumstances shift – and you are in what I should wonder at as the veriest slavery – and I who *could* free you from it, I am here scarcely daring to write . . . I would marry you now. . . .' And at last, on 27 September, Elizabeth surrendered, with one proviso: 'if He should free me within a moderate time from the trailing chain of this weakness, I will then be to you whatever at that hour you shall choose – whether friend or more than friend.' And Browning – '*My own*, now!'

'Why, we shall see Italy together!' he wrote on the last night of October, and on the following day Elizabeth asked. 'When does the book come out?' Then on the 6th, 'dear – dearest – Ever I am yours – The book does not come.' But Browning had just received copies, for on that day ('Bells and Pomegranates VII. Dramatic Romances and Lyrics' was published, a pamphlet of, 24 close-printed pages, scarcely a 'book'.[7] It was dedicated to John Kenyon, paid for by the poet's father, price two shillings a copy. There were 22 poems, five of which, as well as the first nine sections of 'The Flight of the Duchess', had already appeared in *Hood's Magazine*, and most of them were dramatic in the sense of being spoken by imaginary characters, two of them women. As in the *Dramatic Lyrics* of three years earlier, the first thing that strikes the reader, perhaps, is the range of period and place, from sixteenth-century Rome and seventeenth-century Flanders to nineteenth-century Spain; then the range of subject, from Old Testament history to pictures in Florence and poison in Paris. Such variety of matter, grave and gay, romantic, lyrical, satirical, macabre, demands a corresponding variety of manner, and in these poems Browning's technical skill is fully revealed: the steady galloping measure of the ride from Ghent to Aix:

> Not a word to each other; we kept the great pace
> Neck by neck, stride by stride, never changing our place;

the receding music of 'Nobly, nobly Cape Saint Vincent to the North-west died away'; the free rhythm and sometimes fantastic rhyming of 'The Flight of the Duchess':

> And were I not, as a man may say, cautious
> How I trench, more than needs, on the nauseous,
> I could favour you with sundry touches
> Of the paint-smutches with which the Duchess
> Heightened the mellowness of her cheek's yellowness. . . .

That is the Duke's unpleasant old mother, not his young wife, bewitched by the music of the gipsy-woman's voice,

> Till it seemed that the music furled
>   Its wings like a task fulfilled, and dropped
>   From under the words it first had propped,
> And left them midway in the world.

The 'Duchess' was a great favourite with Elizabeth, as well it might be, for the last part is a thinly disguised love poem, the story of a woman who escapes from semi-confinement in her room.

Many of the poems were inspired by Browning's recent Italian visit, 'Pictor Ignotus', for example. The Unknown Painter was one who had failed to move with the times, who 'could have painted pictures like that youth's' – Raphael's perhaps – if he had not kept to the medieval tradition; he had failed, but even his failure had one melancholy consolation:

> If at whiles
> My heart sinks, as monotonous I paint
> These endless cloisters and eternal aisles
> With the same series, Virgin, Babe and Saint,
> With the same cold calm beautiful regard, –
> At least no merchant traffics in my heart.

'The Englishman in Italy' is a description of autumn in the country round Naples, though it finishes with one of Browning's rare references to contemporary English politics:

> Fortù, in my England at home,
> Men meet gravely to-day
> And debate if abolishing Corn-laws
> Be righteous and wise.

Unlike the exuberant Neapolitan harvest of grapes, olives and pomegranates, the prosaic British potato crop of 1845 had failed, and Ireland was threatened with famine, yet there was still a tax on imported grain. The poem's companion piece, 'The Italian in England', is a short dramatic story of an Italian patriot hunted by the Austrians for plotting against their hated rule. And again Browning revealed his heart, this time his support of Italian nationalism against Austrian oppression, symbolised by the reactionary Chancellor Metternich:

> I would grasp Metternich until
> I felt his red wet throat distil
> In blood through these two hands –

though, oddly enough, this was the violent version suggested by Elizabeth instead of his milder 'I felt his throat and had my will.' Perhaps the best, or most enjoyable, of the poems is 'The Bishop Orders his Tomb', in which the old man implores his 'nephews', his illegitimate sons, not to let his dead rival, 'old Gandolf', get the better of him in the tomb:

> And leave me in my church, the church for peace,
> That I may watch at leisure if he leers –
> Old Gandolf, at me, from his onion-stone,
> As still he envied me, so fair she was!

Those last four words, so unexpected, are unforgettable.

On 7 November, after reading the poems, Elizabeth wrote that nobody with an ordinary understanding could any longer complain of obscurity. Yet there were such complaints – 'the mist, if it rises . . . as certainly falls again' – and there were other 'great and obvious faults': carelessness ('rarely careless' was another opinion), verbal vulgarity, musical deficiency. On the whole, however, the few critics who noticed the poems wrote favourably, particularly John Forster: 'freshness of originality . . . melodious transitions of his rhythm . . . delicacy and truth of his genius.' But what pleased Browning best was Landor's tribute in the *Morning Chronicle*:

> Browning! Since Chaucer was alive and hale,
> No man hath walkt along our road with step
> So active, so inquiring eye, or tongue
> So varied in discourse. . . .

It was true: Browning was the Chaucer of another age, or rather, of other ages, and his father was so proud of such praise that he had copies printed as presents for his friends.

And the letters, even longer and more frequent, continued to flow between New Cross and Wimpole Street, followed by locks of hair and lockets, and as a Christmas present Elizabeth signed her letter of 24 December, ' "Love me for ever," as Your *Ba*.' Letters she considered the most vital part of biography, and in her own she certainly gave a lively account of herself and her restricted adventures. She had much to say, of course, about dear Mr Kenyon, and Mrs Anna Jameson now became important in her life. The art critic, formidable champion of women's rights and author of *Shakespeare's Heroines* was an admirer of Browning's poetry as well as that of Elizabeth, to whom she talked about taking her to Italy. There are glimpses of her two sisters, Henrietta and Arabel, to whom she had confided her secret love, of George and her other brothers from whom, for their sake, she had concealed it. They were all dependent on her father, as Henrietta found to her cost when she fell in love, and Elizabeth knew that he would rather see her dead at his feet than married to Browning – or even a prince of Eldorado. There was no question of asking him to meet Robert socially; even George could never bring a friend, and even Mr Kenyon, an old college friend, could not be invited to dinner. 'I am glad,' she confessed, 'I could almost thank God, that Papa keeps so far from me, that he has given up coming in the evening.' And Browning: 'it is SHOCKING.'

As for herself, we learn of her weak eyes: how in broad daylight from a window she saw a man on the other side of Wimpole Street and thought he was Browning, but 'I am so near sighted that I could only see a shadow in a dimness.' She was – half jestingly – a republican, preferred simplicity to high society, and was fascinated by the bohemian way of life. And 'I admire that you, – R.B., – who have had temptation more than enough, I am certain, under every form, have lived in the midst of this London of ours, close to the great social vortex, yet have kept so safe, and free, and calm and pure from the besetting sins of our society.' A great hero-worshipper, she had admired his poetry for years, and it was with pride as well as pleasure that she had received his first letters. Like him, she had a scholarly knowledge of Greek, Latin and French (but not German) literature, which she often quoted, but unlike him knew nothing of painting and pictures, having seen so few, and loving them only as children do, for the sake of the thoughts they bring. 'If ever I am in the Sistine Chapel, it will not be with Mrs Jameson,' but 'what teaching I shall want!' Even better than painting was music, nearest of all arts to poetry, yet her knowledge was limited to the 'private piano'; she had never heard an oratorio in her life – 'judge by that!' Then, she was a mystic, a half-believer in mesmerism, animal magnetism, a craze then at its height; though Browning sturdily maintained that there was no real evidence to warrant belief in such things. More disturbing than mysticism was her addiction to opium, which her doctor made her take to compose her nervous system, and Browning implored her gradually to reduce the doses until she could do without the drug altogether. Neither mesmerism nor opium led to any sort of discord, and the nearest they came to a lovers' quarrel was over the question of capital punishment. Browning: 'I *do* approve of judicial punishment to death under some circumstances – I think we may, *must* say: "when it comes to *that*, we will keep our pact of life, stand by God and put *that* out of us, our world – *it* shall not be endured, or *we* shall not be endured!" ' And Elizabeth: 'Why should we see things so differently, ever dearest? If anyone had asked me, I could have answered for you that you saw it quite otherwise. And you would hang men even – you!'

As a dramatic poet, reluctant to show Elizabeth his *Pauline*, Browning did not often reveal his secret self, save his love, even to her – though he admitted that he had been born 'supremely passionate' – and it was of his outer rather than his inner life that he wrote. Thus: 'holding the volume at a distance which defied my short-sighted eye – all *I* saw was the *faint* small characters.' Then, he was by no means a shunner of society, as he had once described himself: 'I was out last night – to see the rest of Frank Talfourd's theatricals; and met Dickens and his set – so my evenings go away!' We hear of his gardening: planting seven rose-trees one morning and twelve on another; and of his family: of his father studying and illustrating his poems; of his mother, who was 'still suffering sadly', but loved him 'just as much more as must of necessity be'; of Sarianna making fair copies of his manuscripts.

But his main themes were love, marriage, Italy – and health. 'Dear soul of my soul, dearest Ba,' he wrote; and she, 'love me a little, with the spiders and the toads and the lizards! love me as you love the efts.' At the beginning of April he wrote: 'Oh, dearest, let us marry soon, very soon, and end all this.' And she assured him that she would be his 'to go out of England the next half-hour if possible.' Out of England meant Italy: 'when we are in Italy, love. . . . One day we may walk on the galleries round and over the inner court of the Doges' Palace at Venice. . . . When we see the Sistine together.' But all depended on Elizabeth's health: 'Now steadily care for us both . . . walk . . . walk!' And she did, downstairs into the drawing-room, surprising a delighted Henrietta at the piano, and upstairs again, though not yet outside. Her need of opium decreased as her strength increased, 'and every step leads us nearer to *my* "hope".'

Yet he himself was not well, and she in her turn was worried; the pains in his head that began after his return from Italy still plagued him. 'Is it England that disagrees with you?' she asked. 'Did you ever try smoking as a remedy? . . . Then you do not touch wine – and perhaps you ought.' (He assured her that he did sometimes touch wine.) 'Did you ever try putting your feet into hot water at night?' In February he was no better: 'I went out unwell yesterday, and a long noisy dinner . . . have given me such a bewildering headache. . . .' And Elizabeth again: 'I doubt whether the omnibus driving and the noises of every sort betwixt us, should not keep you away for a little while. . . . Would not *riding* be good for you?'

Meanwhile, the day approached for publication of *Luria* in 'Bells and Pomegranates VIII'. Browning had begun the tragedy early in 1845, soon after writing his first letter to Elizabeth, then paused to revise and prepare *Dramatic Romances* for the press; but by mid-November she had the first act, and by the beginning of February the whole play, a 'magnificent work' which the more she read the grander it seemed. But Browning himself was not so sure. 'I am unwell,' he wrote on 23 March, 'and entirely irritated with this sad "Luria" –

I thought it a failure at first, I find it infinitely worse than I thought – it is a pure exercise of *cleverness.*' By this time he had revised another play, *A Soul's Tragedy,* which had lain in his desk for some time, and on 10 March Elizabeth had written: 'for pure nobleness "Luria" is unapproachable. . . . But this "Tragedy" shows more heat than the first . . . it is a great work, and worthy of a place next "Luria".' Browning was unconvinced, and a fortnight later wrote: 'I repeat, both these things, "Luria" and the other, are *manqué,* failures.' And again, on 1 April, when Elizabeth's praise had persuaded him to publish: 'my Ba . . . you have been helping me to cover a defeat, not gain a triumph.' But Elizabeth on the 5th, after reading the proofs: 'To-morrow I shall force you to tell me how you like the "Tragedy" *now*! For my part, it delights me – and must raise your reputation as a poet and thinker.' Then, Browning on the 13th: 'Here . . . comes "Luria" and the other – and I lay it at my dear Lady's feet, wishing it were worthier of them.' Finally, and enchantingly, Elizabeth on the 14th: 'But surely you use too many stamps? Have you a pair of scales like Zeus and me? – only mine are broken.'

'Bells and Pomegranates. No. VIII. and Last' – 'This last attempt for the present at dramatic poetry,' was dedicated in grateful admiration to Walter Savage Landor. And Browning, at Elizabeth's insistence, at last inserted a note to explain his meaning of 'Bells and Pomegranates': 'an alternation, or mixture, of music with discoursing, sound with sense, poetry with thought,' a descriptive summary that readers of the earlier numbers would have found helpful.

The tragedy of Luria, Moor of Florence, was, as Browning himself admitted, inspired by that of Othello, Moor of Venice. Both are simple, loyal, lovable soldiers in the pay of renaissance Italian cities; both are decieved by professed friends, and both commit suicide. But there the resemblance ends, except perhaps for two lines of verse: Othello's 'I have done the state some service, and they know't,' and Luria's unhappy parody, 'I can, and have perhaps obliged the State.' *Othello* is all movement and romantic warmth of passion, but *Luria* is statuesque and classically cold, a tragedy of a single day in five acts without action; instead of a development of the fluidity of *Colombe's Birthday,* a return to the earlier rigidity of speeches a hundred lines long. The reader sympathises with Luria, but is not greatly interested in him or moved by his death, for to kill himself for the possible good of the people of Florence – not 'those old fools i' the council' – is altogether too noble, or, as Elizabeth thought, ignoble. It is significant that the most poignant passage in the play is the Websterian irony of the broken dialogue between Puccio and Luria who has secretely taken poison:

Puccio. Have you a friend to count on?
Luria.   One sure friend.
Puccio. Potent?
Luria.   All-potent.
Puccio.   And he is apprised?
Luria. He waits me.

A Soul's Tragedy – or tragi-comedy – is another tale of sixteenth-century Italy. Luitolfo kills, or thinks he has killed, the tyrannical Provost of Faenza, near Florence, and his remorsefully treacherous friend Chiappino proclaims himself the murderer, only to find that he is a popular hero. Ambition gets the better of him, and in the prose of Act II he is himself about to become Provost when a cheerfully loquacious papal legate arrives, and ensnares, exposes and drives him into exile. Though scarcely the 'great work' that Elizabeth had pronounced it, the 'tragedy' makes an entertaining play for the study if not for performance on the stage, for which it was never intended.

'I shall have my gladness out of the book presently, beyond the imagination of any possible critic,' Elizabeth had written when she received her copy. 'Who in the world shall measure gladness with me?' Very few critics tried. John Forster had some pleasant things to say, and Browning was grateful, but Elizabeth was annoyed that he had scarcely anything to say about *A Soul's Tragedy*; 'Nobody in the world could write such dialogue,' she maintained, and one critic at least agreed that it was 'one of the most intensely dramatic works ever penned.' But if critics ignored the new plays, they aired their views about the 'Bells and Pomegranates' series as a whole, and they were not always complimentary: 'affectation – muddiness of style – muddiness of matter – a sensual trait – themes which had been better left untouched.' Young G. H. Lewes found their author an original thinker and writer, though neither deep nor musical, but Browning's friend H. F. Chorley maintained that his work was full of meaning, sincere and free from affectation, any obscurity being the result of over-accumulation of material. The most percipient judgement, however was William Allingham's: 'the Turner of poetry.' It was true; as Turner had advanced the frontier of painting by interpreting instead of merely reproducing nature, by freeing colour from its restraints, so Browning had advanced, or was advancing, the frontier of poetry by interpreting instead of merely reproducing human nature, by liberating language from the restraints of Victorian romanticism. But at last, at the age of 34, he realised that the formal drama was not his medium, that, as Elizabeth had written a year earlier, 'a great dramatic power may develop itself otherwise.' He had already proved this, but it was to be another ten years before that power was fully revealed. Meanwhile, in the summer of 1846 he paused, as the great adventure of his life approached: Italy with Elizabeth.

Faster and faster flew the letters between New Cross and Wimpole Street, until in June Elizabeth wrote that another would follow again that night: 'Won't that be *three times in a day* according to order ? And Browning: 'I used to see you once a week, to sit with you for an hour and a half – to receive a letter, or two, or three, during the week. . . . Now I see you twice in the week, and stay with you the three hours, and have letter on dear letter.' And at last she began to call him Robert, 'dearest Robert' instead of merely 'dearest'. Then, on the eve of his 34th birthday she wrote that she had not forgotten, and he replied that his birthday was not 7 May 1812 but 20 May 1845, the day on which he had first met her. She had little to say about his work, for he had nothing to show her – 'I never wasted time as at present' – but with reference to her favourite *Soul's Tragedy* she assured him that he had almost thrown off any obscurities of style and had 'a calmer mastery of imagery and language', adding with characteristic modesty that she was merely the fly on the chariot – but, 'How we drive!' She was worried about his health, however, the pain in his head; his mother was ill, and she remembered his 'superstition' of being ill and well with her, to which he replied that the connection between their ailments was no fanciful one. There are glimpses of her sisters and brothers, Henrietta and Arabel, George, now a barrister, 'Stormie' and the rest, who used all to assemble in her room for her half-hour 'Sunday levee" It was Stormie who told her that she had £8000 in the Funds as well as shares in a West Indian ship, though she received from her father only about £180 a year instead of £300 or more. He was another worry, for he was recovering from his anger of the previous year when he had refused to agree to her wintering in Italy, and was again beginning to call her by her old pet names, 'my love', 'my puss', yet now she was planning to escape secretly to Italy with Robert. 'Anything but his *kindness*, I can bear now.' Yet in spite of worries she could jest and laugh: 'I have seen a man, of whom it was related that he *painted his lips* – so that at dinner, with every course, was removed a degree of bloom; the lips paled at the soup, grew paler at the mutton, became white at the fricandeau and ghastly at the pudding – till with the orange at dessert. . . .'

It was George who, after meeting Tennyson at dinner one evening, 'barristerially' compared him with Browning. Was Tennyson an agreeable man, Elizabeth asked, happy in conversation ? 'Yes,' he replied, with grave consideration, 'but quite inferior to Browning. He neither talks so well, nor has so frank and open a manner. The advantages are all on Browning's side, *I should say*.' George was over-solemn, and something of a family joke, but Browning himself gave Elizabeth his opinion of Tennyson after a similar occasion: 'a LONG, hazy kind of a man, at least just after dinner, yet there is something "naif" about him, too, – the genius you see, too.' And he gives us a few rare glimpses of himself. Thus, in reply to a jesting remark by Elizabeth, he wrote in self-defence that he had made himself almost ridiculous by a kind of male prudery with respect to young ladies, having never seen 'any attractiveness in the class'. And again, an explanation that had to be made before their marriage: 'I shall begin by begging a separate room from yours – I could never brush my hair and wash my face, I do think, before my own father – I could not, I am sure, take off my coat before you *now* – why should I ever ?'

Another worry of that summer of anxieties was the suicide of poor Robert Haydon. A friend of Keats and Wordsworth, a megalomaniac who painted huge historical pictures with which he hoped to adorn the walls of the new Houses of Parliament, after some successes he had finally failed, was imprisoned for debt and, aged sixty, shot himself. Elizabeth had never met him, but two years earlier had agreed to store a trunk-full of his journals, and now in his will he asked her to edit them for publication. Apart from their being full of savage remarks about his enemies and rivals, the task was a quite impossible one, but fortunately there was George to give advice, and Serjeant Talfourd, who pronounced them to be the property of Haydon's widow, and on no account to be touched by anybody else.

Although Browning was not well – 'Have you been using the shower-bath ?' – the main anxiety, of course, was Elizabeth's health: 'I expect everything from your going out of doors,' he wrote, and happily the news was progressively encouraging. As early as 16 April she was buying a bonnet, and a month later, when driving in Regent's Park with Arabel and Flush, she got out of the carriage and walked, 'and I put both my feet on the grass, which was the strangest feeling.' Soon she was going out to post her letters to Robert, and walking up the stairs on her return. At the end of May she stood under the green shadow of trees in the Botanical Gardens: 'I never knew before the difference of the *sensation* of a green shadow and a brown one.' In June she drove as far as Hampstead, and at the beginning of July wrote: 'I was out to-day – walked up, walked down, in my old fashion – only I do improve in walking, I think, and gain strength.' A wind still gave her a sort of strangling sensation, 'the effect, I suppose of having weak lungs,' but at the beginning of August Henrietta exclaimed, 'Look at Ba! Did you ever see anyone looking so much better; it really is wonderful, the difference within these few weeks.' No doubt the excitement of unfamiliar experiences was partly responsible for the difference. The organ music in Westminster Abbey both frightened and moved her to tears, 'being so disused to music'; then after driving in Hyde Park on a midsummer evening, 'as we came home, the gas was in the shops – another strange sight for me.' Even stranger was the sight and sound of her first railway engine when 'Mr Kenyon (dear Mr Kenyon in his exquisite kindness!) took me to see the strange new sight (to *me*!) of the Great Western – the train coming in ... and the rush of the people and the earth-thunder of the engine almost overcame me – not being used to such sights and sounds in this room, remember!!'

As Elizabeth's strength increased so did Browning's mention of Italy, though without detailed planning, for she wished to profit as much as possible from the English summer and early autumn; September was the ideal time for their elopement, and impetuous Browning, though chafing at delay agreed. Thus, at the end of May he wrote to say that the English made Florence intolerable, and there was talk of Ravenna, but Elizabeth, consulting a guide-book, suggested Salerno, all fireflies and frogs – 'you will like the frogs' – or Amalfi, where there was a convenient manufactory of maccaroni and writing-paper.

When at the beginning of August she reported that she was now quite well, having had no symptom of illness throughout the summer, the pace quickened. The first question was, where to go? Browning proposed Pisa, from which earthquakes had driven English visitors, making a new lake and sulphurous smoke that rose from rifts in the ground. 'Think!' Elizabeth thought, and agreed. Then, how to get there? They could make the long sea-voyage by way of Gibraltar, or the shorter and cheaper 'land-voyage' through France by river and canal: Havre, Rouen, Paris and the Rhône. Browning's only care was that they should take the less exhausting route for Elizabeth; and she decided: 'let us go through France. And let us go quick, quick, and not stop anywhere within hearing of England. ... May your father indeed be able to love me a little, for *my* father will never love me again.' She had long wondered whether she should tell her father, but knew that his anger would only shake her resolution. She had had to tell her sisters, but had said nothing to Mr Kenyon or Mrs Jameson, for she wished to save them from her father's wrath as accomplices, though they had a shrewd suspicion of what was afoot. And she had told her maid, Wilson, who had agreed to accompany her: an invaluable companion but 'expensive servant – she has sixteen pounds a year.' Then there was Flush – 'you will let him come with us, will you not, dear, dearest?'

And with Flush their troubles began on the first day of September. Browning had warned her about an organised gang that stole dogs and held them for ransom, and that morning Flush was stolen. On the 3rd a man called to demand a ransom of six guineas, but her father ordered him to be turned away, without telling her. Courageously she drove with Wilson to the kidnapper's house in the slums, but it was a week before Flush was returned, thin, thirsty and scared. On the same day, Sunday 6 September, Browning awoke with such pains in his head that he decided to see his doctor, who ordered him to bed on a diet of milk and medicine. 'Do you doubt I shall be well in Italy?' he wrote, but by Wednesday afternoon, though still uneasy in the head, he was well enough to visit her.

That evening, after he had gone, the third blow fell. 'An edict has gone out,' she wrote; her father had decided to take another house for a month or more by the sea or in the country – Dover, Reigate, Tonbridge? – while 50 Wimpole St was repaired and painted. Escape might be almost impossible; 'If we are taken away on Monday, what then?' As soon as he received her note on Thursday morning, Browning told her: 'We must be *married directly* and go to Italy.' He would get a licence, and after all, so he comforted her, the edict had a double advantage: it had precipitated a decision, and the upset of preparation for the move would make it easier for her to pack her luggage without suspicion. So, at 11 o'clock on Saturday 12 September they were married in Marylebone Church, Elizabeth so excited and exhausted that she could barely sign her name in the register.

After the ceremony each returned home, for there was no immediate hurry, the date of the Barrett move having not yet been fixed. By Sunday Elizabeth had recovered sufficiently to write amusingly of a visit from Mr Kenyon in his comically-intimidating spectacles – 'When did you see Browning? . . . When do you see Browning again?' – and Browning himself was able to report: 'Dearest, I woke this morning *quite well* – quite free from the sensation in the head. I have not woke *so*, for two years perhaps – what have you been doing to me?' After months of suspense and inactivity, he had at last been released, and all things were possible. 'I exult,' he cried, and told her how his parents and sister looked forward to meeting her. But Elizabeth: 'I am paralysed when I think of having to write such words as "Papa, I am married; I hope you will not be too displeased".' Meanwhile, there were other letters to be written, one to Mrs Jameson who was in Paris, 'cards' to be printed, and a notice of their marriage inserted in the *Times* after their departure. Then again the pace quickened: this, their elopement, would have to be before Monday 21st, the date suddenly announced for the Barrett move. Browning heard the news on Wednesday 16th, and at once wrote to say that the Havre boat sailed from Southampton on *Wednesdays* and *Saturdays*, and that he was taking only a portmanteau and carpet-bag. It would have to be Saturday, Elizabeth hesitatingly replied: 'Wilson and I have a light box and a carpet-bag between us. ... Do you take a desk?' On Thursday morning he told her that the sailings had been changed, that the boat left on *Tuesdays* and *Fridays*, but discovered his mistake in time to catch the evening post; he had confused the sailings from Havre with those from Southampton. But now he made another muddle, this time about trains from London to Southampton, but Elizabeth saw his error: 'Surely you say wrong in the hour for to-morrow. Also there is the express train. Would it not be better?' It was 11.30 on Friday morning when Browning wrote his last letter: 'How thankful I am you have seen my blunder ... What I shall write now is with the tables before me. ... The packet will leave to-morrow evening from the Royal pier, Southampton at *nine*. We leave Nine Elms, Vauxhaull, at *five* – to arrive at *eight*. I shall be at Hodgson's *from* half-past three to *four precisely* when I shall hope you can be ready.' And Elizabeth, that night: 'At from half-past three to four then. ... Is this my last letter to you, ever dearest? Oh – If I loved you less .. a little, little less.' So on Saturday afternoon, 19 September 1846, Elizabeth, Wilson and Flush slipped quietly out of Wimpole Street to join Browning on their flight to Italy.

II. FLORENCE 1846–1861

5. *Casa Guidi*

1847–55

AFTER what must have been a physical as well as spiritual ordeal for Elizabeth, the Brownings reached Paris where they found Mrs Jameson, who was as eager to help as delighted to see them. Fortunately she was herself on the way to Italy with her niece, and insisted on being their guide. So, by way of Orleans the party of four women, one man and a dog made their way down the Rhône valley, then sailed to Genoa and Leghorn, where they took a train for the last few miles to Pisa. There Mrs Jameson left them, a little anxious about their future: Elizabeth was desperately tired after her long journey, and though Browning was a genius in high spirits, the best of travelling companions, he was the least practical of men in mundane affairs.

They took comfortable rooms near the Cathedral, where they passed the winter in seclusion, Browning doing his best to cheer Elizabeth, and leaving her only to take exercise or when asked to do so when she had bad news from England, a reproachful letter from George, her own letters to her father returned unopened, and information that he had thrown her possessions into boxes and sent them to a warehouse, for the storage of which she was to pay. Despite this, she wrote cheerfully to Miss Mitford that Robert was all tenderness and goodness. that Pisa was delightful and the climate mild in spite of the rain, and that, although Robert was not greatly interested in novels, in a story for a story's sake, they were reading together Stendhal's *Rouge et Noir*. That was in February 1847, but a month later she was taken ill, and it was only after a visit from a doctor that she discovered the reason. She had a miscarriage but, to the wonder of Wilson, Robert nursed her so devotedly that within a few days she recovered and was able to report that never before had she felt so well.

Soon afterwards they moved to Florence, where they found spacious and airy rooms with a balcony on which they could sit in the heat of summer eating water-melons, figs and all manner of fruit. In June, however, they tried to escape to Vallombrosa, in the hills some miles east of Florence, where there were eagles but no roads. 'Robert went on horseback,' Elizabeth wrote to Miss

Mitford, 'and Wilson and I were drawn on a sledge – (i.e. an old hamper, a basket wine- hamper– without a wheel) by two white bullocks, up the precipitous mountains. Think of my travelling in those wild places at four o'clock in the morning!' They had hoped to stay two months at the monastery, 'but the new abbot said or implied that Wilson and I stank in his nostrils, being women. So we were sent away at the end of five days. So provoking! Such scenery, such hills.' A year later she commemorated the event in verse:

> And Vallombrosa, we two went to see
>   Last June, beloved companion, – where sublime
> The mountains live in holy families. . . .
>   The Vallombrosan brooks were strewn as thick
> That June-day, knee-deep, with dead beechen leaves,
>   As Milton saw them, ere his heart grew sick
> And his eyes blind. I think the monks and beeves
>   Are all the same too.

The lines come from *Casa Guidi Windows*, for in April 1848 they had moved into rooms in the Casa Guidi on the west side of the river Arno, opposite the Piazza and Palazzo Pitti.

The year 1848 had dawned peacefully over Europe, but the calm was deceptive, for it was to prove the Year of Revolutions. Marx and Engels were writing their *Communist Manifesto* with its final slogan, 'Workers of the world, unite!' though it was not for communism that the people rose, but for political reform and freedom from foreign domination. Britain was a fortunate exception, for the Corn Laws had been repealed, the Whigs were in power, a period of reform, free-trade and prosperity was beginning, and the last demonstration of the Chartists ended in laughter when their gigantic petition was found to be signed seventeen times by the Duke of Wellington as well as by 'Victoria rex, April 1st'. Ireland after its famine was another matter, but an attempted revolution was easily crushed.

It was very different on the continent of Europe. In February France expelled its king and again became a republic; there were risings in Berlin and Vienna, from which Metternich fled, while the Czechs of Bohemia and Magyars of Hungary rose against Austrian rule, and in Italy, Ferdinand of Naples, the new Pope Pius IX, the Grand Duke Leopold of Tuscany, and Charles Albert of Piedmont all granted constitutional reform. In March the Milanese drove the Austrian troops out of their city, as did the Venetians, who declared their territory a republic. Charles Albert now assumed leadership of the Italians in their struggle against Austria, though half-heartedly, for kings are not enthusiastic supporters of republican revolutions. Defeated at Custozza in July, he was compelled to withdraw from Milan, and agree to an armistice that left the Austrians masters again of Lombardy.

A few days before the battle the Brownings had left Florence for a holiday at Fano on the Adriatic coast. It was intolerably hot, but, wrote Elizabeth, 'the churches are very beautiful, and a divine picture of Guercino's is worth going all that way to see.' No doubt she was quoting Browning, for he paid three visits to the church of San Agostino to see this seventeenth-century painting of an angel holding a small child's hands in prayer. It is an oddly decadent, sentimental picture for an original, unsentimental poet to have admired, but he saw it, as somewhat shamefacedly he wrote later, 'in a favourable *darkness*', and he was interested in Guercino as a painter who had helped to introduce him as a boy to Italian art in the Dulwich Gallery. After three days in Fano they fled a few miles farther down the coast to Ancona, where he wrote 'The Guardian Angel', the first poem he is known to have written since his marriage, and one of the worst that he ever wrote – or published: conventional Victorian sentiment in conventional 'poetic' manner – 'wouldst thou . . . when thou hast done' – inspired by the intense religiosity of his own 'angel', Elizabeth. But then, he was not well when he wrote.

By the late autumn, when they were back in Florence, the critical scene of the Risorgimento had shifted to Rome where, in November, the Pope's minister Rossi was murdered, and Pope Pius fled to Naples and the protection of 'Bomba', King Ferdinand, who had bombarded his subjects into submission. Then, in February 1849 Rome was declared a republic under Mazzini, who was joined by Garibaldi and his band of volunteers. In December, however, Louis Napoleon, nephew of the late Emperor, had been elected President of the French Republic, and, an opportunist posing as defender of Europe from revolutionary socialism, in April he sent troops to take Rome. After a heroic defence the city fell at the end of June, and Garibaldi found refuge in America, Mazzini in England.

So the old forms of reactionary government were restored in Italy: Ferdinand in Naples, Pope in Rome, Austrians in Lombardy and Venetia, Grand Duke Leopold in Tuscany, which, like Rome, had from February to June been a republic. But not in Piedmont. There, after a second defeat by the Austrians at Novara in March, Charles Albert had abdicated in favour of his son Victor Emmanuel who, with his minister Cavour, awaited the opportunity to unify Italy under the crown of Piedmont.

From Casa Guidi windows Elizabeth saw and heard the early enthusiasm of the Tuscans and wrote exultingly, '*O bella libertà, O bella!*' but later when she saw the failure of her hopes and Leopold restored by the Austrians, she wrote of the Florentines:

> If we did not fight
> Exactly, we fired muskets up the air
> To show that victory was ours of right.

And of

> stifled Rome,
> Dazed Naples, Hungary fainting 'neath the thong,
> And Austria wearing a smooth olive-leaf
> On her brute forehead, while her hoofs outpress
> The life from these Italian souls. . . .
> Why, almost through this Pius, we believed
> The priesthood could be an honest thing, – he smiled
> So saintly while our corn was being sheaved
> For his own granaries!

And in 'Old Pictures in Florence' Browning was soon to write of the octogenarian Radetzky, Austrian commander at Custozza and Novara, and now Governor of Lombardy-Venetia:

> When the hour grows ripe, and a certain dotard
> Is pitched, no parcel that needs invoicing,
> To the worse side of the Mont Saint Gothard,
> We shall begin by way of rejoicing;
> None of that shooting the sky (blank cartridge). . . .

He too must have seen from Casa Guidi windows Leopold's restoration in May 1849, but it was Elizabeth who described it:

> From Casa Guidi windows gazing, then,
> I saw and witness how the Duke came back.
> The regular tramp of horse and tread of men
> Did smite the silence like an anvil black
> And sparkless. With her wide eyes at full strain,
> Our Tuscan nurse exclaimed, 'Alack, alack,
> Signora! these shall be the Austrians.' 'Nay,
> Be still,' I answered, 'do not wake the child!'
> – For so, my two months' baby sleeping lay
> In milky dreams upon the bed and smiled.

For, after more miscarriages, on 9 March 1849, three days after her own forty-third birthday, Elizabeth had given birth to a son.

For Elizabeth the strain of her long labour had been mainly a physical one, for Browning a spiritual anguish, and their reaction was correspondingly joyful when they found their child to be a normal and healthy boy. He was christened Robert Wiedemann Barrett, though he soon became 'Penini', then simply 'Pen', the name by which he was always to be known. Mr Kenyon's birthday present was £100 a year for his parents, and Browning sent a lock of the child's hair to his mother. She did not see it, for she died a week after her grandson's birth. From joy Browning was plunged into the deepest grief, for the bond between son and mother was abnormally strong, even their health seeming to vary in sympathy; for the first thirty-four years of his life Browning had rarely been parted from her, and he felt that his flight with another woman was in the nature of a betrayal. Nearly two months later Elizabeth wrote: 'He has loved his mother as such passionate natures only can love, and I never saw a man so bowed down in an extremity of sorrow.'

Browning's depression continued; he could not bear the thought of returning home with all its old associations – 'Here's the garden she walked across, / Arm in my arm, such a short while since' – and it was only Elizabeth's insistence that the baby must escape from the summer heat of Florence that induced him to move. They found comfortable rooms at the Baths of Lucca, near Pisa and the sea, and there Browning's spirits began to improve, as did Elizabeth's health. She had never felt so well, and there was one memorable expedition when she, Wilson and the nurse ('with baby') on donkeys, Browning on horseback, rode five miles into the mountains 'not far from the stars'. And it was in Lucca, perhaps in an attempt to cheer him, but mainly because he had said 'something against putting one's love into verse', that she said shyly one morning: 'Do you know I once wrote some poems about *you* ?' and put into his hands a sheaf of forty-four sonnets that she had written during the months of his visits to Wimpole Street.

They are not very good sonnets, partly because they are written in the Italian form with its exacting repetition of rhyme – all very well in Italian, but not so well in almost rhymeless English – and rhyme was not one of Elizabeth's strong points. Unlike Browning, she was a better writer of prose than of verse; her letters are full of sly humour, courageously high spirits and vivid description, but these sonnets are often embarrassingly self-conscious and stilted in expression – 'Thou, bethink thee, art' – and almost as embarrassing in their frequent morbidity. And yet they are affecting as well as interesting: a sick and lonely woman's exaltation at finding that she is loved, loved by such a man as Browning, the unrestrained expression of her own love, and her so womanly

93

humility. Sonnet 23 is one of the best, perhaps the one that most haunted Browning in after years:

> Is it indeed so ? If I lay here dead,
> Wouldst thou miss any life in losing mine ?
> And would the sun for thee more coldly shine
> Because of grave-damps falling round my head ?
> I marvelled, my Belovëd, when I read
> Thy thought so in the letter. I am thine –
> But .. so much to thee ? Can I pour thy wine
> While my hands tremble ? Then my soul, instead
> Of dreams of death, resumes life's lower range.
> Then, love me, Love! look on me – breathe on me!
> As brighter ladies do not count it strange,
> For love, to give up acres and degree,
> I yield the grave for thy sake, and exchange
> My near sweet view of Heaven, for earth with thee!

Browning was overwhelmed, love blunted his critical faculty: Elizabeth was the better poet, and it was owing to him that the sequence was included in a second edition of her *Poems* in 1850, though with the deliberately misleading title of 'Sonnets from the Portuguese'.

Browning himself had been preparing a two-volume edition of his own collected poems, published in 1849, though without *Pauline* and the disastrous *Sordello*. It had involved a good deal of revision, but he had written almost nothing new since the spring of 1846 when he had publsihed *Luria*. Since then, for the first time in his life, he had had responsibilities: preparations for his secret marriage and flight to Italy, care of an invalid wife, a household to manage, and finally a child to look after. But now his mother's death and Elizabeth's love-sonnets compelled him to write, and under the influence of these two devout nonconformist women, with vividly revived memories of his chapel upbringing and Elizabeth's summary of her faith in a letter written shortly before their marriage –

> I believe in what is divine and floats at highest in all these different theologies – and because the really Divine draws together souls, and tends so to a unity, I could pray anywhere and with all sorts of worshippers . . . but . . . I like, beyond comparison best, the simplicity of the dissenters –

in December 1849 he began to write *Christmas Eve*.

Elizabeth, who secretly disapproved of the theatre, had urged him to abandon the formal drama and write dramatic poetry that was not intended for the stage: admirable advice; but most of all she wanted him to write a long

On Saturday, at St. Marylebone Church, by the Rev. Thomas Wood Goldhawk, M.A., Robert Browning, Jun., Esq., of New-cross, Hatcham to Elizabeth Barrett, eldest daughter of Edward Moulton Barrett, Esq of Wimpole-street.

8. From *The Times*, 21 September 1846.

9: Elizabeth Barrett Browning in 1850, when restored to health by her marriage and the birth of Pen. Crayon drawing by Lowes Dickinson. *Courtesy Armstrong Browning Library.*

10. Casa Guidi: 'the doorway where the black begins
With the first stone-slab of the staircase cold.'
Armstrong Browning Library.

poem about himself, his own philosophy, his own beliefs: 'let us have your own voice speaking of yourself.' Less admirable advice, for *Christmas Eve* is in a sense a return to *Pauline*, a confession, the kind of poem that he had avoided since that first ill-fated publication – 'all my poetry is dramatic' – though with a difference: *Pauline* was a boy's apology for his lapse into atheism, *Christmas Eve* was to be a man's account of his Christian creed. The poem, some 1400 octosyllabic lines, was finished early in the new year, and immediately followed by another 1000 lines on *Easter Day*, the two being published together shortly before Easter 1850.

Christmas Eve is an elaboration of Elizabeth's creed. On the Christmas-Eve of 'Forty-nine' Browning visits in imagination a seedy nonconformist chapel in London, but the 'immense stupidity' of the preacher so revolts his reason that he falls asleep. In a dream he is whisked off to St Peter's in Rome, where this time the splendid ritual of the Pope's celebration of Mass obscures the essence of Christianity – love. Swept off to Göttingen he hears a rationalist lecturer whose cult of reason has left only the ghost of love. Finally he wakes to find himself still in the London chapel, and decides that if he must choose a place for worship it is here in the simplicity of nonconformism.

There are fine descriptive passages in the poem, notably that of the moon-rainbow on his flight to Rome, but best of all are the racy Chaucerian-Dickensian sketches of the men and women he sees:

> the fat weary woman
> Panting and bewildered, down-clapping
> Her umbrella with a mighty report,
> Grounded it by me, wry and flapping,
> A wreck of whalebones; then, with a snort,
> Like a startled horse. . . .

> He pushed back higher his spectacles,
> Let the eyes stream out like lamps from cells,
> And giving his head of hair – a hake
> Of undressed tow, for colour and quantity –
> One rapid and impatient shake. . . .

The poem would have been far more effective, however, if Browning himself had preached less; prose, not verse, is the proper medium for sermons, and though most people would agree that love, or at least altruism, is the basic virtue, few would agree, as he seems to imply, that it is almost exclusively a Christian ideal.

On the whole, however, *Christmas Eve*, as befits the season it celebrates, is a tolerant, even genial poem, but *Easter Day*, again perhaps in accord with the season, is dry and austere. There is no comic relief: the couplets are regular octosyllabics, instead of wildly-rhyming hudibrastics, and there are no men and women, only two anonymous speakers, Browning and another – and God. It begins as a dialogue on the theme how very hard it is to be a Christian, but then becomes a non-dramatic monologue when Browning describes a vision, real or imaginary, of Easter 1846. As he was crossing the common by the chapel, he seemed to feel the Judgement-Day begin, and then,

> A final belch of fire like blood,
> Overbroke all heaven in one flood
> Of doom. Then fire was sky, and sky
> Fire, and both, one brief ecstasy,
> Then ashes. But I heard no noise
> (Whatever was) because a voice
> Beside me spoke thus, 'Life is done,
> Time ends, Eternity's begun,
> And thou art judged for evermore.'

He was, he found, shut out of heaven; he had enjoyed the world too much, so – ' 'Tis thine for ever – take it!' Rejoicing in his wealth, he decides to seek happiness in nature, but what, asks the Voice, are the beauties of this earth compared to those of heaven? So, despite short despairs,

> Henceforth my part
> Be less with nature than with art!
> For art supplants, gives mainly worth
> To nature; 'tis man stamps the earth –
> And I will seek his impress, seek
> The statuary of the Greek,
> Italy's painting – there my choice
> Shall fix!

Again the scornful Voice, and in anguish he cries,

> Mind, the mind. . . . Mind is best –
> I will seize mind, forego the rest.

'And so much worse thy latter quest,' echoes the Voice. So finally in desperation:

> I let the world go, and take love!
> Love survives in me, albeit those
> I love be henceforth masks and shows,
> Not living men and women. . . .
> I pray, –
> Leave to love, only!

' 'Tis somewhat late!' cries the Voice severely, but the poem ends with the dreamer's prayer and its acceptance:

> 'Only let me go on, go on,
> Still hoping ever and anon
> To reach one eve the Better Land!'
> Then did the form expand, expand –
> I knew Him through the dread disguise,
> As the whole God within his eyes
> Embraced me.

Although the Oxford Movement may be said to have ended in 1845 with Newman's secession to Rome, controversy was still raging within the Church of England when *Christmas Eve and Easter Day* was published five years later. Manning was about to follow Newman's example, and there was considerable opposition to the restoration of the Roman Catholic hierarchy in England when Wiseman was appointed cardinal and first Archbishop of Westminster. Browning's reference to 'Rome's gross yoke', therefore, might have been expected to please Nonconformists and Low Churchmen, but if so they scarcely trumpeted their approval. It is true that the dissenting John Forster praised the poems for their mastery of thought, emotion and language, but he had to admit that the message was sometimes a little narrow and intolerant. Browning had yet to win his laurel and be recognised as one of the most original poets of his time. There was qualified praise in a few other reviews, but on the whole they were distinctly unfavourable – 'grotesque', 'rhyming eccentricities', 'mystical' – and the muscular protestant Charles Kingsley entered the lists and, quoting Browning's 'how can I help England?' told him: 'By leaving henceforth "the dead to bury their dead," in effete and enervating Italy.' Even Elizabeth complained of the asceticism of *Easter Day*.

Only a few hundred copies were sold. It was another failure, but not altogether Browning's fault. Although he was a sincere Christian, he was anything but the ascetic of *Easter Day*; still shaken by the death of his so dearly loved mother, it was her voice speaking through him, and he still needed time to recover, to rediscover the other delights of his boyhood and youth experienced in his father's library: the whimsical conversation and drawings and shelves of humanist books.

When not on holiday during the Florentine summer, the Brownings lived quietly at Casa Guidi, the rooms of which they gradually filled with old furniture and pictures that were to be had cheaply if looked for. They avoided the ordinary English residents and tourists eager to see the famous poet

Elizabeth Barrett, and Browning rarely or never left her in the evening, though more and more frequently they were visited by newly-made friends. In the summer, however, they left Florence again, this time for Siena, the medieval Ghibelline city among the Tuscan hills, where Browning, as a Florentine Guelph, must have thought ruefully of *Sordello*. Shortly before their arrival Wordsworth had died, and the question of a new Poet Laureate arose. There was some talk of Elizabeth for the post: a woman would be the more appropriate Laureate for a Queen. But there could be little doubt about the final decision; Tennyson had just published *In Memoriam*, and he was appointed. There was no mention of 'the author of *Paracelsus*'.

It was now more than four years since the couple had left England, and in 1851, the year of the Great Exhibition in Hyde Park, they decided, in spite of misgivings – his mother's garden, her father's anger – that they ought to return and introduce Pen to their families. They went by way of Venice, which roused Elizabeth to ecstasy, while Pen grew gloriously fatter, but Robert was unwell, nervous, unable to eat or sleep, and Wilson even worse: 'Alas for these mortal Venices, so exquisite and so bilious.' So by way of Milan, where Elizabeth climbed to the roof of the cathedral, they made for Paris and London, which they reached in July. There Wilson left them to go to see her mother in Yorkshire, leaving Elizabeth to look after, and to spoil, Pen. They took rooms near Portman Square, only a few hundred yards from Wimpole Street, with the intention of soon moving to New Cross. Elizabeth was understandably nervous, and her London cough returned. She did not dare to visit her father, and when she and Robert wrote imploring him to see his grandson, he sent a violent reply to Robert with a bundle of the letters that she had written to him during the five years since their marriage, '*unopened, the seals unbroken*'. Henrietta had recently married Captain Surtees Cook and, like her, had been disowned, so that Elizabeth's visits to Wimpole Street with Pen were confined to the times when her father was out, and they could be lovingly received by Arabel, and even by George and her other brothers.

They were, of course, welcomed at New Cross, where Elizabeth met her father-in-law and Sarianna for the first time, but they did not, after all, stay there, partly, perhaps, because Browning found memories of his mother too oppressive, partly because the village, though fast becoming a suburb, was too far from the social centre. After a five-years' absence Browning naturally wanted to see old friends again. First of all there was their benefactor, dear Mr Kenyon, then old Samuel Rogers, elderly 'Barry Cornwall', and among his contemporaries, Joseph Arnould, John Forster and Tennyson, and one of the first he went to see was Carlyle, now aged 56 and preparing to write his *History of Frederick the Great*. Mrs Carlyle was unimpressed, but the two men were devoted friends, each admiring the other's work, and when the Brownings left for Paris in September, a London winter being too great a risk for Elizabeth, Carlyle accompanied them, for he could speak no French, and Browning's services proved invaluable.

The little family – Robert, Elizabeth, Pen, Flush – now rejoined by Wilson, found comfortable sunny rooms in the Champs Elysées. After five years of near solitude with an invalid wife, albeit much recovered, reunion with father and sister, renewal of old friendships and social life in London, had so revived Browning's health and spirits that at last he felt able, impelled, to settle down for the winter and write, not verse to begin with, but prose – an essay on Shelley.

He was soon interrupted, however. 'Robert's father and sister have both been paying us a visit during the last three weeks,' Elizabeth wrote on 12 November. 'They are very affectionate to me, and I love them for his sake and their own.' But she did not mention the reason for their visit. Perhaps she did not know. Mr Browning, now nearly seventy, had been making an ass of himself and writing passionate love-letters to a neighbouring twice-married widow with three children, a Mrs von Müller; but doubts had recently risen and damped his ardour. He did not, of course, tell his son details of his infatuation, but simply that he was being persecuted by a scheming woman. Browning, therefore, wrote an indignant letter to Mrs Müller, and his father followed it with another saying that he had broken off the engagement owing to her former misconduct – scarcely a letter to put into the hands of a scheming woman. So Browning's father and sister returned to London, leaving him free to finish his essay on Shelley.

He wrote at the request of his former publisher, Edward Moxon, who wanted it as an Introduction to some newly-discovered letters of Shelley – all but two of which were soon to be proved forgeries – and Browning, remembering his mother's unwittingly giving him a copy of Shelley's 'atheistical poem' *Queen Mab*, and anxious to make amends, willingly accepted the offer. The result was an oddly perverse attempt to show that Shelley, a sincere, tender, generous, sympathetic young man, could not have been at heart an atheist, but was essentially a Christian, on the verge of declaring his faith when he was drowned. Browning knew, for he himself had once professed atheism. But he knew little about the life of his so compassionate hero: that his wife Harriet Westbrook, whom he had married when she was 16, had drowned herself three years later when he left her for Mary Godwin.

Nor will men persist in confounding, any more than God confounds, with genuine infidelity and an atheism of the heart, those passionate, impatient struggles of a boy towards distant truth and love, made in the dark, and ended by one sweep of the natural seas before the full moral sunrise could shine out on him. . . .

I shall say what I think, – had Shelley lived he would have finally ranged himself with the Christians; his very instinct for helping the weaker side (if numbers make strength), his very 'hate of hate', which at first mistranslated itself into delirious Queen Mab notes and the like, would have got clearer-sighted by exercise. . . .

It is because I have long held these opinions in assurance and gratitude, that I catch at the opportunity offered to me of expressing them here. . . .

Paris, Dec. 4th, 1851.

The day on which Browning finished his essay was a sinister one in French history. Louis Napoleon's term of office as President of the Second Republic was almost over, and as he was not eligible for re-election and the Chamber refused to alter the Constitution, he himself changed it by arresting his opponents during the night of December 1st, and appealing to the people On the 4th there was fighting in Paris, when his troops shot some two hundred republicans, but the country voted overwhelmingly in favour of his *coup d'état* and the extension of his Presidency. Exactly a year later the Man of December was proclaimed Emperor – Napoleon III.

Elizabeth's latest poem had just been published, though it was not through Casa Guidi windows that she and Browning saw the all-but-Emperor's triumph of December 1851, but from their balcony in the Champs Elysées. Oddly enough, she hailed as prospective saviour of Italy the man who had crushed the short-lived Roman Republic and restored the Pope, describing how he rode through Paris 'in the name of the people', and a few years later hailed him

> Emperor, Emperor!
> From the centre to the shore,
> From the Seine back to the Rhine,
> Stood eight millions up and swore
> By their manhood's right divine
>   So to elect and legislate,
> This man should renew the line
> Broken in a strain of fate
> And leagued kings at Waterloo,
> When the people's hands let go.
>   Emperor
>   Evermore.

For Browning, however, the man was a renegade, an opportunist, the 'wretched impostor' of his satirical *Prince Hohenstiel-Schwangau*, 'Saviour of Society', begun at about the same time as Elizabeth's tribute. Napoleon III was a subject on which they never agreed; but then, Elizabeth did not live to see the decline and fall of the Second Empire.

Having finished his essay on Shelley, Browning was eager to turn again to verse which, apart from *Christmas Eve and Easter Day*, for some six years he had so neglected that he resolved to make amends by beginning the year 1852 with a poem a day. On New Year's Day, therefore, he wrote 'Women and Roses' which, he said, was suggested by a magnificent basket that some one had sent his wife. The poem is a dream of three roses each circled by women, one by those long dead, another by the living, the last by those yet to be born: the sort of theme that was to be so characteristic of the verse – and prose – of Thomas Hardy, a boy of only eleven when Browning wrote:

> Round and round, like a dance of snow
> In a dazzling drift, as its guardians, go
> Floating the women faded for ages,
> Sculptured in stone, on the poet's pages.
> Then follow women fresh and gay,
> Living and loving and loved to-day.
> Last, in the rear, flee the multitude of maidens,
> Beauties yet unborn. And all, to one cadence,
> They circle their rose on my rose tree.

After the dream a nightmare: 'Childe Roland to the Dark Tower Came', a poem, Browning said, that he had to write 'then and there', and finished in one day. The immediate source was Edgar's line in *King Lear*, adapted from the ballad of 'Child Roland and Burd Ellen', but the hopeless journey across a stricken plain may well have been a medley of memories, conscious and unconscious, from childhood onwards. Browning always maintained that it had no conscious allegorical significance, yet the forlorn mysterious quest is an emblem of the spiritual courage that he so much admired; and the conclusion, as Roland is watched by all the other lost adventurers, is triumphant:

> There they stood, ranged along the hill-sides, met
> To view the last of me, a living frame
> For one more picture! in a sheet of flame
> I saw them and I knew them all. And yet
> Dauntless the slug-horn to my lips I set,
> And blew. *"Childe Roland to the Dark Tower came."*

Thirty years later Van Gogh was to discover and depict the beauty of ugliness:

Robert Browning

'Places as hideous as possible are for the artist a paradise. . . . How beautiful the mud is, and the withered grass.' But Browning had anticipated him:

> As for the grass, it grew as scant as hair
> In leprosy; thin dry blades pricked the mud
> Which underneath looked kneaded up with blood.
> One stiff blind horse, his every bone a-stare,
> Stood stupefied, however he came there.

The landscape of 'Childe Roland' is as hideous as possible, and not the least of Browning's achievements was the extension of the frontier of his art by transforming unrelieved ugliness into poetry.

After the nightmare another dream-like poem followed on the third day of the year – 'Love among the Ruins'. It is both Italy remembered and a vision of the Italy of the mysterious pre-Roman Etruscans, the remains of whose highly-developed civilisation were then being excavated and for the first time revealed to the modern world: peaceful pastures now overlying and concealing the ruins of splendid palaces. It is also a love poem, and Browning concludes:

> Oh heart! oh blood that freezes, blood that burns!
> Earth's returns
> For whole centuries of folly, noise and sin!
> Shut them in,
> With their triumphs and their glories and the rest!
> Love is best.

And the poem itself is among the best that Browning wrote, the metrical form that he invented of alternating long and chiming short lines so perfectly, and hauntingly, suiting the subject.

It was a splendid start to the new year, but the pace was too exhausting to keep up, and Paris had its distractions. One of these was George Sand. Elizabeth greatly admired the work of this passionate woman novelist of about her own age, and thanks to a letter of introduction she and Robert secured an invitation to visit her in her bed-sitting room, after which they met several times. Elizabeth liked her, and even defended her cigarette-smoking as a feminine weapon; 'a noble woman under the mud', she concluded. But Browning had his reservations, disliking, as she did, the admirers who surrounded her, smoking, spitting, ill-bred men 'of the ragged red, diluted with the low theatrical.'

Joseph Milsand was a very different matter. A scholar with an exceptional knowledge of English, he had just published a perceptive essay on Browning's poetry in the *Revue des Deux Mondes*, which led to a deep and lasting friendship between the two men, and when *Sordello* was at last republished in 1863 it was dedicated to 'J. Milsand, of Dijon.' Perhaps it was after reading that puzzle that he remarked, 'What an extraordinary man! His centre isn't in the middle.' Elizabeth quite loved him, not only for his interest in Pen, but also as a perfect creature who 'always stands in the top place among our gods.'

They returned to London in the early summer, and again met old friends and made new acquaintances. There was William Fox who had so generously helped Browning in his youth, and of course Carlyle, who introduced them to Mazzini. And there was young Rossetti, son of another exiled Italian patriot, and one of the founders of the Pre-Raphaelite Brotherhood. A poet as well as a painter – his 'Blessed Damozel' had recently appeared – he was a great admirer of Browning's work, read *Sordello* aloud to the Brotherhood, and had written to ask Browning if he was right in thinking that the anonymous *Pauline* was his. The Pre-Raphaelites were bitterly attacked by some critics, but cautiously defended by Ruskin, whom Browning now met for the first time, thus beginning another long friendship.

The delights of the London season were darkened, however, when Browning heard that Mrs von Müller was bringing an action for breach of promise against his father. He was not present in court when the case was heard on 1 July, but on the next day he read the report in *The Times*, and for the first time heard the full extent of his father's folly. There were letters beginning 'My dearest, dearest, dearest, dearest, dearest, dearest much-loved Minny', and defending counsel could only plead that they were those of 'a besotted old man' in a case that recalled 'Bardell v. Pickwick'. As his salary was stated to be about £320 a year, damages of £800 were awarded to Mrs Müller, and Browning and Sarianna were left to comfort their father as best they could. 'Robert has been to see his father,' Elizabeth wrote to Mrs Jameson, 'and held the grey head on his shoulder and loved and pitied him.' Robert himself was in need of comfort, for 'he could scarcely raise his head after the blow of that dreadful newspaper.' But it was not only the publicity that upset him, it was also, mainly perhaps, his father's betrayal of his mother.

The £800 penalty, nearly three years' salary, was a crippling one, and rather than attempt to pay it Mr Browning decided to seek refuge in Paris. Robert accompanied him, and found rooms in which he left him in tolerable comfort before returning to London after an absence of only three days, when he and Sarianna began the melancholy and wearisome labour of disposing of their father's house and furniture. Sarianna then joined her father in Paris, while Robert, physically and spiritually exhausted, resumed his social life in London.

A few weeks later the Duke of Wellington died, and Tennyson wrote his Funeral Ode: 'Bury the great Duke / With an empire's lamentation.' Then, on 6 October Mr Kenyon gave the Brownings a farewell dinner-party, after which Crabb Robinson joined them: 'I found an interesting person I had never seen before, Mrs Browning, late Miss Barrett – not the invalid I expected; she has a handsome oval face, a fine eye, and altogether a pleasing person. She had no opportunity of display, and apparently no desire. Her husband has a very amiable expression. There is a singular sweetness about him.'[8] A few days later they were in Paris, where they found a chastened and apologetic Mr Browning well cared for by Sarianna and some English friends, and by the beginning of November they were back in Casa Guidi.

After nearly eighteen months of travel and society, Elizabeth was understandably glad to be back in the restful seclusion of Florence, but Browning who enjoyed these things found the place dull, at least for a time. Soon, however, he settled down to a routine: writing in the morning, walking and looking at old pictures in galleries and churches in the afternoon, and in the evening reading about their painters in Vasari's *Lives of the Artists*. Travel had stimulated him; he was writing as he had not written for years, and at the end of February 1853, nearly four months after their return, he told Joseph Milsand: 'I have not left the house one evening since our return. I am writing – a first step towards popularity for me – lyrics with more music and painting than before, so as to get people to hear and see.' Elizabeth, too, was working hard, beginning her long blank-verse romance of *Aurora Leigh*.

There was one interruption, however. Helen Faucit, now Mrs Martin, who had played the lead in *Strafford* and *A Blot in the 'Scutcheon*, asked permission to produce the yet unacted *Colombe's Birthday*, which Browning willingly gave, and in April it had a run of seven performances at the Haymarket. Elizabeth heard a report of 'the miserable acting of the men. Miss Faucit was alone in doing us justice.' Yet the critics who saw it were more generous: Although 'a charming poem rather than a drama', Miss Faucit was able to make the audience understand the story, and the production was a great success. John Forster was more explicit, more penetrating. Browning was a dramatic poet rather than a dramatist; his characters never go out of their way to explain their situation or themselves, and as these things have to be inferred from what they say, subtleties often become obscurities when the lines are spoken by an actor.

Although Browning did not see it, the production renewed his interest in the drama, and the result was another play, *In a Balcony*, interesting mainly as a reversal of the theme of *Colombe's Birthday*. In this a Duchess falls in love with one of her subjects and all ends happily, but in the other a Queen falls in love with one of her subjects, but finds that he loves another woman, and the play ends with the tramp of approaching guards. *In a Balcony*, a very short play, was not intended for the stage; if it had been, Forster's remarks on *Colombe's Birthday* would again have been pertinent, for Browning was in no hurry to make clear the situation: that Norbert wishes to tell the Queen of his love for Constance, and her reason for dissuading him, a situation that must have been prompted by memories of his own secret courtship of Elizabeth, when Mr Barrett played, or almost played, the part of the Queen.

Browning may have written or finished the play at the Baths of Lucca to which they went again for three months in the late summer. And there, with his wife and two small children, was the young American sculptor William Story whom they had met in Florence in 1848, before he established himself in Rome where his studio soon became a centre for those interested in the arts. 'Our friends Mr and Mrs Story help the mountains to please us a good deal,' Elizabeth wrote. 'We go backwards and forwards to tea and talk at one another's houses.' There were also expeditions into the mountains, the ladies on horseback, notably one to Prato Fiorito 'six miles there and six miles back, perpendicularly up and down,' an excursion that inspired the writing of one of Browning's finest love poems, 'By the Fireside'. Written probably after their return to Casa Guidi, it is a quiet poem of deep emotion recollected in tranquillity, memories of their expedition mingled with memories of their early love, and of the peaceful evenings of the previous winter by their fireside:

> My perfect wife, my Leonor,
> Oh heart, my own, oh eyes, mine too ..
> Reading by fire-light, that great brow
> And the spirit-small hand propping it. ....

Elizabeth is loving and faithful as Leonora-Fidelio of Beethoven's opera, and Browning's meeting with her and her love for him make his youth seem almost a waste in comparison with the present:

> Oh, the little more, and how much it is!
> And the little less, and what worlds away!
> How a sound shall quicken content to bliss,
> Or a breath suspend the blood's best play,
> And life be a proof of this!

The following months were not to be altogether as idyllic as anticipated. In

November they had an 'exquisite' week's journey to Rome, by way of Assisi and the great waterfall near Terni, entering Rome at evening in the highest of spirits, 'Robert and Penini singing'. The Storys had taken an apartment for them, and all was ready for their arrival, but on the next morning came the news that their son was ill, and the Brownings spent their first day in Rome beside a dying boy. His sister, too, almost died of the same disease, gastric fever, and other members of the Story family were afflicted by the, less deadly, Roman fever. No wonder Elizabeth, thinking of Pen, wrote in January 1854: 'All this has blackened Rome to me. I can't think about the Caesars in the old strain of thought.'

There were compensations, however, among them being the daughters of Charles Kemble: the older, Fanny, of about Elizabeth's age and the most famous actress of her day, and her sister Mrs Sartoris, a promising opera singer before her retirement after marrying a wealthy Italian. 'Mrs Sartoris' house has the best society in Rome,' wrote Elizabeth, 'and exquisite music of course.' But Fanny was her favourite, though 'somewhat unelastic. . . . She thinks me credulous and full of dreams.' It was true: Elizabeth was credulous, a mystic. Unable to bear the thought of death, annihilation – 'When I look deathwards I look *over* death, and upwards' – she now turned to spiritualism for support of her craving for survival. Spiritualism was sweeping the United States at this time. It had begun in 1848 with the Fox family of daughters in New York, whence the medium Mrs Haydon had sailed to England in 1852, and in this year 1854 young Daniel Home was also preparing to export his séances to London. As there were many American residents and visitors in Rome, Elizabeth was able to indulge her passion for the occult, to discuss messages from the dead and even take part in séances, in table-tapping and mysterious disturbances of furniture. Browning would have nothing to do with these things, and while she whispered to spirits he chatted to ladies, one of whom was Thackeray's daughter Anne, who vividly described him at this time, aged nearly forty-two, as 'a dark short man, slightly but nervously built with a frank open face, long hair streaked with grey and a large mouth which he opens widely when he speaks, white teeth, a dark beard and a loud voice with a slight lisp, and the best and kindest heart in the world.'

But spiritualism was reserved for the evenings, and in the daytime there were other forms of entertainment, including expeditions and picnics in the Roman countryside with the Kemble sisters and their friends. After one of these picnics the party broke up and its members strolled away, all but Elizabeth who was too tired to move, and Browning, as was his custom, stayed with her, a kindness that led Fanny Kemble to remark later that he was the only man she had ever known who behaved like a Christian to his wife. It was a memory of this or some other expedition that prompted the writing of 'Two in the Campagna', in which Browning expressed a man's desire for complete spiritual union with the woman he loves. Sometimes for a moment he achieves it, but

> Then the good minute goes.
> Already how am I so far
>   Out of that minute?. . . .
> Just when I seemed about to learn!
> Where is the thread now? Off again!
> The old trick! Only I discern –
>   Infinite passion, and the pain
> Of finite hearts that yearn.

It is a lovely though enigmatic lyric; it may be dramatic, as he maintained all his poems were, but 'By the Fireside', of the same period, certainly is not, and 'Two in the Campagna' reads more like Browning addressing Elizabeth in a moment of dejection.

'To leave Rome will fill me with barbarian complacency,' she wrote in May. The death of the young Story boy still haunted her, and she was naturally worried about Pen: 'my child, the light of my eyes, has been more unwell than I ever saw him.' They were back in Florence before the end of the month, with the intention of going to Paris and London in the summer. But they had no money – Mr Kenyon was apt to forget his annual contribution – and they had much work; Elizabeth had not yet finished *Aurora Leigh*, nor were the manuscripts of Browning's poems yet ready for the publisher. And then, the Crimean War had begun.

As Russia had long wanted an outlet in the Mediterranean, she picked a quarrel with Turkey whose decaying empire blocked the way, but France and Britain, fearful of Russian expansion, supported the Turks. By September the fighting was concentrated in the Crimean Peninsula on the Black Sea, where Russia was building a naval base at Sebastopol, and there followed the battles of the Alma, Balaclava (celebrated by Tennyson in his 'Charge of the Light Brigade') and Inkerman as preludes to the siege of the fortress during the dreadful winter of 1854–55. Fortunately Florence Nightingale arrived in November to organise a hospital for the frost-bitten wounded men, and in the New Year the incompetent British government was succeeded by a more efficient one under Palmerston. At the same time Cavour and Victor Emmanuel, seeing their chance of being reckoned a power in Europe and of making a long stride towards the unification of Italy, joined the allies, and by April thousands of Piedmontese troops had joined the French and British in the Crimea – events that the Brownings followed with more than common interest and excitement.

If the war had anything to do with their delay, its end was now in sight, and by the summer they were in Paris, where Wilson married their Italian man-servant. They were joined by Sarianna on the last stage of their journey to London, which they reached in July and at last Browning was able to deliver his manuscripts to his publishers, Chapman and Hall. Despite the pleasure of seeing old friends like Mr Kenyon and Carlyle and again meeting Ruskin whom they liked very much and whose Turner paintings they admired, the visit was not a great success. After Florence, Elizabeth detested the rainy English summer; then in August Mr Barrett packed off his family to East-bourne while the Wimpole Street house was decorated again, and Pen, without Wilson, went with them. And there was no Browning house at New Cross, no gentle Mr Browning to be visited.

There was, however, the medium Daniel Home, the 22-year-old American who had just arrived in London to begin a lucrative career in spiritualism. As Elizabeth longed to attend one of his séances, Browning agreed to take her to see one of his performances at the house of some friends. The most memorable item of the proceedings was the raising from the table round which they were seated of a garland of clematis which, guided by spirit hands, settled on Elizabeth's head. Browning disliked Home and the whole business, shortly afterwards writing that he could scarcely understand how there could be another opinion than his own on the matter, 'that the whole display of "hands", "spirit utterances", etc, were a cheat and imposture.' And when Home called to see Elizabeth at their Dorset Street lodgings he told him so, for he was understandably angry and worried by this exploitation of an excitable invalid-woman's credulity. Spiritualism was to remain a subject on which Browning profoundly disagreed with Elizabeth, and a few years later he was to vent his feelings in verse – in 'Mr Sludge, "The Medium" '.

By the beginning of September the proof-sheets of his poems had arrived for his correction, and on the 22nd he added the final 'One Word More. To E.B.B.' as a dedication to Elizabeth. A few days later Tennyson came to dinner, smoked his pipe and, wrote Elizabeth to Helen Faucit, 'opened his heart to us (and the second bottle of port), and ended by reading *Maud* through from end to end and going away at half past two in the morning.' She did not add that her husband followed the Laureate with a reading of his yet unpublished

'Fra Lippo Lippi'. 'Maud' had been published in July, since when thousands of copies had been sold, and one can understand Browning's thoughtful expression in the portrait by Rossetti, who was also at the reading, making sketches of the poets.

Another month and the Brownings were back in Paris, in uncomfortable rooms (without Wilson whom they had left in England with a baby son) waiting anxiously for news of the publication and reception of *Men and Women*.

6. 'Men and Women'
1855–56

PUBLICATION and reception came together on 17 November 1855. 'Energy wasted and power misspent . . . obscurity . . . wilderness of mist and of sand.' And a week later: 'This sort of thing should be stopped . . . madness and mysticism . . . nonsensical book.' It is not easy for us, living more than a century after the appearance of *Men and Women*, after a revolution that has affected all the arts both in matter and manner, a revolution of which Browning was a main leader, it is not easy for us fully to understand the impercipience of mid-Victorian reviewers. 'The manner will be newer than the matter,' Browning had written to Forster, 'I hope to be listened to this time.' But the matter was often as new (or strange) as the manner. What was a reviewer to make of the 51 lines of 'Transcendentalism: A Poem in Twelve Books'? Yet it is almost a key-poem, the one that Browning chose as introduction to the twelve dramatic monologues that he called 'Men and Women' when he rearranged his work for the collected edition of 1863.[9]

Transcendentalism was a philosophy much in vogue at this time in New England, where Emerson was one of its exponents, and in Old England, or Scotland, Carlyle: a philosophy that maintained that knowledge derived from the physical senses is limited, and that true knowledge is intuitive, or supernatural. Browning does not deny this, but he tells a brother poet that Transcendentalism is not a subject for Twelve Books of didactic verse:

> Song's our art. . . .
> Stark-naked thought is in request enough:
> Speak prose and hollo it till Europe hears! . . .
> But here's your fault; grown men want thought, you think!
> Thought's what they mean by verse, and seek in verse.
> Boys seek for images and melody,
> Men must have reason – so, you aim at men.
> Quite otherwise!

Even Shakespeare's German contemporary Jacob Boehme – how many reviewers knew the works of Boehme? – described in his dry-as-dust prose how he once heard flowers talking, but John of Halberstadt 'vents a brace of rhymes / And in there breaks the sudden rose herself,'

> Buries us with a glory, young once more,
> Pouring heaven into this shut hour of life.
> So come, the harp back to your heart again!

A strange message from the man whose last publication had been *Easter Day*, who was to write 'A Poem in Twelve Books', the 21,000 lines of *The Ring and the Book*, and a few weeks after publication of *Men and Women* wrote to tell Ruskin that 'poetry is all teaching.' So, in a sense it is, but not overt teaching, not preaching, and happily there is little preaching in *Men and Women*. That 'A poet's affair is with God,' as he also informed Ruskin, is another matter, a matter of opinion with which his young contemporaries Swinburne and Hardy, would scarcely have agreed; but while writing these poems Browning was under the influence of two very religious women, a mother whom he had rarely left until she died shortly after his carrying off to Italy a wife whose side he never left. As a result the poems of 1855 might almost be called 'Men and Women and God', but, again fortunately, the best of them are concerned with flesh and blood, with living or once living, real or imaginary, men and women. They are also Browning at his best, at the peak of his career, which means that they are, many of them, among the great poems in our language.

The title may have been suggested by a line from the Sonnets that Elizabeth had given him shortly after his son's birth and mother's death in 1849, for No. 26 must have been much in his mind:

> I lived with visions for my company
> Instead of men and women, years ago,

until, that is, she met her Beloved, a man who put her dreams to shame. As might be expected, most of the poems are about Italy, many of them about Renaissance painting and sculpture, and some about music. Most of them are dramatic in the sense that not Browning but the characters speak, women as well as men. It follows that there are no conventional verse-forms, no sonnets, no odes, and few developed similes, but instead there is great variety of mood, grave and gay, tragic and humorous, with a corresponding metrical variety, rising or falling, racy or meditative measures, from blank verse to unrhymed trochaics, from *terza rima* to outrageously rhyming hudibrastics, and all informed by an energy, exuberance, confidence, either patent or restrained.

The first poem was the recently written 'Love among the Ruins', the love-poem to Elizabeth, non-dramatic, though none was to know it, and most suitable of all as an introduction to the series that finished with the dedicatory epilogue of 'One word More'. In the collected edition of 1863 it was one of the thirty 'Men and Women' poems that Browning re-classified as 'Dramatic Lyrics', a misleading title, for a lyric is a short personal poem intended for music, and few of these 'dramatic lyrics' are obviously associated with song. 'Misconceptions' is exceptional, a true lyric that has been set to music, and an exquisite example of Browning's pure poetry:

> This is a spray the Bird clung to,
>   Making it blossom with pleasure,
> Ere the high tree-top she sprung to,
>   Fit for her nest and her treasure.
>   Oh what a hope beyond measure
> Was the poor spray's, which the flying feet hung to, –
> So to be singled out, built in, and sung to!

'Saul', on the other hand, is dramatic, spoken by David, yet lyrical in the sense that he recounts the song that he sang to restore the afflicted and speechless King. The first nine sections had appeared ten years earlier in *Dramatic Romances*, but since then the beginning had been given a middle and an end, a unity that made it twice as long again. The earlier part is the better, for soon after that, owing to Elizabeth who had persuaded him to make the addition, overt teaching, preaching, begins; not at once, however, and the long simile, again exceptional, at the beginning of the tenth section is equal to anything that had gone before:

> 'Saul!' cried I, and stopped,
> And waited the thing that should follow. Then Saul, who
>   hung propped
> By the tent's cross-support in the centre, was struck by
>   his name.
> Have ye seen when Spring's arrowy summons goes right to
>   the aim,
> And some mountain, the last to withstand her, that held
>   (he alone,
> While the vale laughed in freedom and flowers) on a broad
>   bust of stone
> A year's snow bound about for a breastplate, – leaves
>   grasp of the sheet?
> Fold on fold all at once it crowds thunderously down to
>   his feet,

And there fronts you, stark, black, but alive yet, your
    mountain of old,
With his rents, the successive bequeathings of ages
    untold. . . .
                                 One long
    shudder thrilled
All the tent till the very air tingled, then sank and
    was stilled
At the King's self left standing before me, released and
    aware.

Very different is 'Master Hugues of Saxe-Gotha', in which an organist left
alone in his candle-lit loft asks the shade of the composer Hugues what he
meant by the fugue he has just played to the departed congregation. 'Is it your
moral of life?'

> Seems it surprising a lover grows jealous –
>   Hopes 'twas for something his organ-pipes sounded,
>   Tiring three boys at the bellows?

Different again is the pathos of 'A Toccata of Galuppi's', gay, lightly-touched
clavichord music that evokes visions of young 18th-century Venetians taking
their pleasure 'when the sun was warm in May,' yet music that also seems to
foretell that soon they will be nothing but dust and ashes:

> Dear dead women, with such hair, too – what's become
>   of all the gold
> Used to hang and brush their bosoms?

Music and women's hair: quintessence of Browning.

Of the original fifty poems of *Men and Women* twelve were later added to
the *Dramatic Romances*, one of them being the nightmare-like 'Childe Roland'.
Another, so grotesquely original, so Browningesque, that it could scarcely be
mistaken for any other man's work, was 'Holy Cross Day', the day when Jews
in Rome were compelled to attend a Christian sermon. 'What the Jews really
said, on thus being driven to church,' wrote Browning, 'was rather to this
effect:–'

> Fee, faw, fum! bubble and squeak!
> Blessedest Thursday's the fat of the week.
> Rumble and tumble, sleek and rough,
> Stinking and savoury, snug and gruff. . . .

Scarcely an introduction acceptable to reviewers in the decade of *Idylls of the
King*. Yet another very original poem, both in matter and metre, is 'A Grammarian's Funeral', in which Browning imagines an early-Renaissance scholar's

devotion to learning, one who would learn how to live before living, a contrast to the gay Venetians of Galuppi's day:

> Others mistrust and say, 'But time escapes:
> Live now or never!'
> He said, 'What's time? Leave Now for dogs and apes!
> Man has Forever.'

Two of these romances are of contemporary life, but 'The Last Ride Together' combines the themes of Galuppi and the Grammarian. A rejected lover persuades his mistress to take one last ride with him, life indeed, not a shadow of life like art – and 'Who knows but the world may end to-night?' Or even,

> What if we still ride on, we two. . . .
> And heaven just prove that I and she
> Ride, ride together, for ever ride?

'The Patriot' is a satirical comment on the revolutionary triumph and failure of 1848–49, when the fickle Florentines exchanged roses for stones to throw at their leader, but in 'The Statue and the Bust' Browning returned to sixteenth-century Florence and the legend of how, through procrastination, lack of determination, the Duke and a newly-married lady failed to become lovers in deed as well as desire. 'And the sin I impute to each frustrate ghost,' Browning startlingly concluded,

> Is – the unlit lamp and the ungirt loin,
> Though the end in sight was a vice, I say.
> You of the virtue (we issue join)
> How strive you? *De te, fabula.*

Scarcely a moral acceptable to mid-Victorian reviewers.

Perhaps the best of the eight poems that remained as 'Men and Women' after the rearrangement of 1863 are 'Andrea del Sarto', 'Fra Lippo Lippi' and 'Bishop Blougram's Apology.' The first two are the fruit of Browning's exploration of Florentine picture galleries and churches, and his reading of Vasari's *Lives of the Artists*. They are true dramatic monologues, in the first of which del Sarto, 'the perfect painter', pleads with his faithless wife Lucrezia to encourage him in his work, for with her help 'We might have risen to Rafael, I and you!' The verse could scarcely be simpler, more lucid, and it is full of realistic touches that bring the characters to life: Lucrezia's not listening when Andrea tells her of Michelangelo's praise of his work, her smearing one of his paintings as she passes. It is a grey melancholy poem of failure to develop to the full; he is the perfect but earth-bound craftsman, not the soaring inspired artist that he might have been. Others, inferior craftsmen

> Reach many a time a heaven that's shut to me. . . .
> Ah, but a man's reach should exceed his grasp,
> Or what's a heaven for?

Elizabeth was the reverse of Lucrezia, the perfect partner who encouraged and inspired, and the lines are a curious, probably unconscious, variation on a passage in one of her early love-letters: 'One's ideal must be above one, as a matter of course, you know. It is as far as one can reach with one's eyes (soul-eyes), not reach to touch.'

'Fra Lippo Lippi' was the poem that Browning read after Tennyson's reading of 'Maud' at the party that he gave shortly before publication of *Men and Women*. A fine contrast to 'Andrea del Sarto', it is a breezy, colloquial almost-autobiography of the early fifteenth-century painter whom Browning saw as the man who broke away from medieval conventions to paint real men and women – as he himself broke away from Victorian romanticism to write about them. 'Paint the soul, never mind the legs and arms,' the Prior insists; but Lippi, the realist and worldly friar:

> Or say there's beauty with no soul at all –
> (I never saw it – put the case the same –)
> If you get simple beauty and nought else,
> You get about the best thing God invents.

And he runs back to his room in the house of his patron Cosimo of the Medici, from which he escaped for a night's revel with the girls: 'There's the grey beginning. Zooks!'

In 'Bishop Blougram's Apology' Browning skips four centuries, from 1450 to 1850, for Blougram is a caricature of Cardinal Wiseman, the first Roman Catholic Archbishop of Westminster. Browning obviously liked poor Brother Lippi, whose worldliness was not in the least worldly ambition, but simply a break from work and an inspiration of his art; but Blougram is a calculating churchman who enjoys the good things of this world – riches, comfort, power – and believes, or half-believes, because it certainly pays in this world and probably will pay in the next. Moreover,

> Let us concede (gratuitously though)
> Next life relieves the soul of body, yields
> Pure spiritual enjoyment: well, my friend,
> Why lose this life i' the meantime, since its use
> May be to make the next life more intense?

So Blougram, believing half he speaks in his monologue over the port, quite confounds poor Gigadibs, the unbelieving literary man; but amusing as he is in his casuistry, he talks too much and becomes something of a bore. However, he remains in possession of the dinner-table, driving Gigadibs to Australia to replenish it.

'Blougram' is a satirical portrait of a successful half-believer, but two of the dramatic monologues, or rather monographs – if the usage be allowed, for both are letters – treat of men who would, or might, have believed whole-heartedly in Christianity if they had had the opportunity. 'An Epistle of Karshish' is an engagingly simple account of an Arab physician's journey to Jerusalem where he meets 'one Lazarus' who claims that he has died, been buried, and restored to life by a Nazarene physician:

> This man so cured regards the curer, then,
> As – God forgive me! who but God himself. . . .
> Why write of trivial matters, things of price
> Calling at every moment for remark?
> I noticed on the margin of a pool
> Blue-flowering borage, the Aleppo sort,
> Aboundeth very nitrous. It is strange!. . . .
> The very God! think Abib; dost thou think?
> So, the All-Great, were the All-Loving too. . . .
> 'But love I gave thee, with myself to love,
> And thou must love me who have died for thee!'
> The madman saith He said so: it is strange.

Blougram had little or nothing to say about love, but for Browning love was the very core and essence of Christianity, and the simpler the form of worship the less was it obscured or diluted by irrelevant cermonial.

In 'Cleon' the scene shifts to Greece, though Cleon the poet is a contemporary of Karshish the man of science. A master of all the arts and eminently successful, he still finds something lacking, something that is essential to happiness:

> In man there's failure, only since he left
> The lower and inconscious forms of life. . . .

(A remarkable anticipation of Darwinism)

> I dare at times imagine to my need
> Some future state revealed to us by Zeus,
> Unlimited in capability
> For joy, as this is in desire for joy. . . .
>   But no!

Zeus has not yet revealed it; and alas,
He must have done so, were it possible!

As a postscript he adds that he has heard of Christus and Paulus, probably the same man, but how can a mere barbarian Jew have access to a secret hidden from the civilised Greeks?

And (as I gathered from a bystander)
Their doctrine could be held by no sane man.

So to the epilogue of 'One Word More' dedicating the poems to E.B.B.

Love, you saw me gather men and women,
Live or dead or fashioned by my fancy,
Enter each and all, and use their service,
Speak from every mouth, – the speech, a poem. . . .
Let me speak this once in my true person.

As a unique celebration of his love, Raphael exchanged painting for poetry, and wrote a century of sonnets to his Margherita; for the same reason Dante changed his medium and, instead of writing a poem, painted a picture of his Beatrice. But, Browning wrote to his Elizabeth, he had nothing but verse to offer her, yet 'He who writes may write for once as I do,' that is, blank verse with a reversed rhythm, falling trochaics instead of rising iambics, a unique celebration of his love, for it is a metre peculiar to this poem. So,

There they are, my fifty men and women
Naming me the fifty poems finished!
Take them, Love, the book and me together:
Where the heart lies, let the brain lie also.

'Robert's poems are magnificent,' Elizabeth had written to her married and disinherited sister Henrietta at Taunton, and a few days after their publication reported that Joseph Milsand considered them 'superhuman': 'Mark that! Only superhuman.' But the professional reviewers continued to rate them as mortal indeed, if not subhuman: 'harsh, obscure, perverse', 'slipshod familiarities', 'keen enjoyment of dirt'. Some wrote more in sorrow than in anger: 'a fine mind enfeebled by caprice', 'a careless strength'. Even George Eliot, after praising his freshness, originality, robust energy and courage, concluded that his great deficiency was want of music: 'though Browning never flounders helplessly on the plain, he rarely soars above a certain table-land – a footing between the level of prose and the topmost heights of poetry.' Carlyle, too, had his reservations; he wrote a kind letter praising the keenness of his insight, and 'fresh valiant manful character, equipped with rugged humour,

with just love, just contempt. . . . But what is the shadow side of the picture ?
. . . "unintelligibility!". . . . A writing man is there to be understood.' Then,
in his just published fourth volume of *Modern Painters* Ruskin, citing 'The
Bishop Orders his Tomb', praised Browning as 'unerring in every sentence he
writes of the Middle Ages . . . in those seemingly careless and too rugged
lines of his,' and now, after reading *Men and Women*, he wrote to ask him to
explain himself. Having at last found more comfortable rooms in Paris,
Browning replied on 10 December:

I cannot begin writing poetry till my imaginary reader has conceded licences
to me which you demur at altogether. I *know* that I don't make out my conception by my language, all poetry being a putting the infinite within the finite.
You would have me paint it all plain out, which can't be; but by various
artifices I try to make shift with touches and bits of outlines which *succeed*
if they bear the conception from me to you. You ought, I think, to keep pace
with the thought tripping from ledge to ledge of my 'glaciers', as you call them;
not stand poking your alpenstock into the holes, and demonstrating that no
foot could have stood there; – suppose it sprang over there ? In *prose* you may
criticise so – because that is the absolute representation of portions of truth,
what chronicling is to history – but in asking for more *ultimates* you must
accept less *mediates*, nor expect that a Druid stone-circle will be traced for you
with as few breaks to the eye as the North Crescent and South Crescent that
go together so cleverly in many a suburb. . . .

Do you think poetry was ever generally understood –or can be ? Is the
business of it to tell people what they know already, as they know it, and so
precisely that they shall be able to cry out – 'Here you should supply *this* –
that, you evidently pass over, and I'll help you from my own stock' ? It is all
teaching on the contrary, and the people hate to be taught. They say otherwise,
– make foolish fables about Orpheus enchanting stocks and stones, poets
standing up and being worshipped, – all nonsense and impossible dreaming.
A poet's affair is with God, – to whom he is accountable, and of whom is his
reward; look elsewhere, and you will find misery enough. Do you believe
people understand *Hamlet* ?. . . .

I look on my own shortcomings too sorrowfully, try to remedy them too
earnestly: but I shall never change my point of sight, or feel other than dis-
concerted and apprehensive when the public, critics and all, begin to understand and approve me. But what right have *you* to disconcert me in the other
way ?. . . .

Take my truest thanks, and understand at least this rough writing, and, at
all events, the real affection with which I venture to regard you. And 'I' means
my wife as well.[10]

Ruskin was impressed, though he did not ask Browning what he meant by a
poet's affair being with God, how he knew, but sent him an inscribed copy of

his last book as a Christmas present. It was acknowledged at once, though by Elizabeth from their new address at 3 Rue du Colysée, for it was evening, and Robert dressing to go out on an engagement. And she added a postscript, quoting 'Time's Revenges' of ten years earlier: 'So it was true – was it? –

> I've a friend over the sea;
> I like him, but he loves me.
> It all grew out of the books I write.'

Browning was 43, Ruskin 36, Carlyle 60, and it is significant that the most enthusiastic, unqualified praise of *Men and Women* came from young poets of the next generation. Thus, 21-year-old William Morris placed Browning 'high among the poets of all time, and I scarce know whether first, or second, in our own: and it is a bitter thing to me to see the way in which he has been received by almost everybody.' And 27-year-old Rossetti wrote to William Allingham: 'What a magnificent series is *Men and Women!*'

Of course it is. Exactly ten years earlier Landor had compared Browning to Chaucer, as active, inquiring and perceptive, as varied in discourse, and if that was true of the *Dramatic Romances* it was even truer of *Men and Women*. There were 29 Pilgrims, men and women, who rode out of the stableyard of London's Tabard Inn on that memorable April morning of 1387, but 50 Men and Women emerged from a London publishing house in November 1855. It is true that there was no Harry Bailly, no Host, to gather them together and act as guide and master of ceremonies, for each went his own way and had his own, not another's, story to tell. Nor was there any prim Prioress or jolly Wife of Bath in the company; but Blougram, Lippo Lippi, del Sarto, Karshish, Cleon, Childe Roland, the organist of 'Master Hugues' and soliloquiser on Galuppi would, or should, all have been in the running for the free supper promised by Harry Bailly to the teller of the best tale. Browning's range of character and story was even wider than Chaucer's, for Chaucer died a few years before the birth of Lippo Lippi, the man who, according to Browning, brought realism into painting, as Chaucer brought it into medieval poetry, and Browning himself into that of the Victorian age. He is not as racy as Chaucer, nor is his comedy so broad, so outrageously funny, but there is humour and high spirits as well as pathos, and tragedy beyond the range of Chaucer; and he has a far greater dexterity in verse forms that are themselves creative of character – but then, he lived more than two centuries after Shakespeare, Chaucer more than two centuries before. He is not, however, as endearing, as companionable as the poet who laughed at himself as well as at others, who allowed himself to be thus described by Harry Bailly:

> He in the waist is shape as well as I;
> This were a poppet in an arm t'embrace
> For any woman smal and fair of face;

the poet who told the boring jog-trot story of 'Sir Thopas', told it until stopped:

> 'By God,' quod he, 'for pleynly, at a word,
> Thy drasty rymyng is nat worth a turd!'

and ordered to tell another tale *in prose*. On the other hand Browning had a greater lyrical gift, though he did not often practise it, for both poets were above all interested in men and women, Browning in what they think rather than in what they do, in motive rather than action, and both shared the inquiring mind of Shakespeare.

'Do you think poetry was ever generally understood?' Browning asked Ruskin. 'Do you believe people understand *Hamlet*?' Shakespeare is obscure because of his profundity, Chaucer because of his old-fashioned (though not really difficult) English, Browning because he assumes that his readers are as knowledgeable and intelligent as himself. Even to Ruskin he had to explain his poem 'Popularity', which finishes:

> Hobbs hints blue, – straight he turtle eats:
>   Nobbs prints blue, – claret crowns his cup:
> Nokes outdares Stokes in azure feats, –
>   Both gorge. Who fished the murex up?
> What porridge had John Keats?

Yet in the preceding verses he had made it clear that the murex is a shell-fish and the source of a blue dye, Tyrian purple, and the last verse simply means that the discoverers, innovators, creators (Keats) die in poverty, while the exploiters of their genius (Hobbs, Nobbs and the rest) live in luxury. And how true that is!

The trouble was that *Sordello* of 1840, which might have been another murex, had proved a millstone, so that 'Browning' had become almost synonymous with 'obscurity', and the critics of 1855, instead of seizing on bright and obvious beauties, were still poking about in search of anything not easily understood; and Browning wrote to his publisher Edward Chapman: ' "Whoo-oo-oo-oo" mouths the big monkey – "Whee-ee-ee-ee" squeaks the little monkey and such a dig with the end of my umbrella I should give the brutes if I couldn't keep my temper, and consider how they miss their nut and gingerbread!' Chapman could offer little comfort, for after a brisk start sales rapidly declined, and Browning, disappointed and depressed by the reception of what he knew to be his best and most important work, wandered about Paris or sat at home quite unable to write. Encouraged by Elizabeth, he tried for a time to revise *Sordello*, make it more comprehensible, then joined his father in copying pictures in the Louvre – a sad decline for the author of 'Andrea del Sarto' and 'Fra Lippo Lippi'.

Meanwhile Elizabeth was working hard at *Aurora Leigh*, when not petting and spoiling Pen, whose seventh birthday they celebrated in March 1856. The poem was nearly finished by June when they returned to London where, before it was sent to the publisher, Browning read it as a whole for the first time, and wrote on the manuscript: 'Read this Book, this divine Book, Wednesday night, July 9th, 1856. – R.B., 39 Devonshire Place.' The address was that of Mr Kenyon, who had gone to the Isle of Wight for the sake of his health, for he was very ill, and insisted on the Brownings staying in his princely London home. While there they met Nathaniel Hawthorne at one of Monckton Milnes's famous breakfast-parties, and Hawthorne was impressed by Browning, both by his good looks and simple, agreeable manner. However, when Mr Barrett heard of their arrival in London he packed off the remains of his family again, this time – happily – to the Isle of Wight, to which the Brownings followed them, and were thus able to visit Mr Kenyon as well. On their way back to London in September they stayed with Henrietta at Taunton, and by October were again in Florence waiting for news of *Aurora Leigh*.

7. End of an Act
1856–61

THEY had not long to wait, and on 18 December Rossetti wrote to Allingham: 'The piece of news freshest in my mind is *Aurora Leigh*, – an astonishing work surely. . . . Oh, the wonder of it! . . . The Brownings are long gone back now, and with them one of my delights, – an evening resort where I never felt unhappy. How large a part of the real world, I wonder, are those two small people? – taking meanwhile so little room in any railway carriage, and hardly needing a double bed at the inn.' The poem is the autobiography of Aurora Leigh (with a touch of Elizabeth Browning's) who eventually marries her philanthropic cousin Romney, though the real heroine is a tramp's daughter, Marian Erle, who, rather than degrade Romney socially, abandons him at the last moment. But the story is scarcely 'dramatic' in Browning's sense of the word, and is little more than a pretext for the expression of Elizabeth's own views on society, morality, art and religion. Although there are interesting and pathetic passages, it is in the main either didactic or Victorian melodrama, and it is difficult to understand why Rossetti should have thought it so wonderful, Browning so divine, and Ruskin 'the greatest poem in the language'. A few critics disagreed, finding it vulgar or positively indecent, but most of them praised the poem extravagantly and, to Browning's joy and Elizabeth's surprise, it was soon in its 5th edition. Meanwhile, sales of *Men and Women* had virtually ceased, except in the United States, where there was no copyright law, and from which therefore came no royalty payments. Robert Browning was little more than Elizabeth Barrett's husband.

Shortly before leaving London she had dedicated her poem to her 'cousin and friend' John Kenyon, from his house in Devonshire Place, but soon after its publication came news of his death. It is odd that Elizabeth, who believed so passionately in a new and better life to come, should have been so affected by death; but then, it was Elizabeth she mourned for: never again would she see and enjoy the society of dear Mr Kenyon. There were compensations, however; thanks to West Indian investments, he was a very wealthy man, and

to Elizabeth he left £4,500, to Robert £6,500. For Browning, who up till now –
he was 44 – had been dependent first on his father then on Elizabeth, the
bequest was a tremendous relief and, though it made little difference to their
way of life, they could now afford unaccustomed luxuries, one of which, for
Browning, was riding. And Pen, they now knew, was well provided for.

They spent the winter of 1856–57 in Florence, and then in April Elizabeth
received a letter to say that her father had died. It was ten years since she had
last seen and spoken to him, ten years since she had left the affectionate-
tyrannical patriarch of Wimpole Street for another man, and all that time
she had reproached herself for her desertion; grief was now added to accumu-
lated remorse, and for a month she was so prostrated that she was unable to
leave Casa Guidi. Browning looked after her, and as soon as she was well
enough took her to the Baths of Lucca for the summer. There they were
joined by their young admirer Robert Lytton, future Viceroy of India
(ironically enough, it was the summer of the Indian Mutiny), son of Bulwer-
Lytton whose successful plays had been partly responsible for the failure of
Browning's. Isabella Blagden also came, a kindly, intelligent, lively woman, a
writer who let rooms to her friends in her villa at Bellosguardo, (mentioned in
Aurora Leigh) on the outskirts of Florence. But the holiday was not a great
success: Lytton was stricken with gastric fever, and for weeks Browning helped
Isa Blagden to nurse him, before he had to look after Pen who went down with
the same disease. And Elizabeth was not well.

Browning, however, was in good spirits, spending the winter of 1857–58 at
Casa Guidi looking after her and her affairs, teaching Pen, visiting artists'
studios, studying anatomy – he bought a skeleton – modelling and drawing,
though apparently not painting. The Hawthornes arrived in the spring and
were impressed by his exuberance and vitality, though they thought they could
detect a trace of anxiety for his wife, who seemed too frail to live much longer.
However, she was well enough to go to Havre in the summer, where they were
joined for a time by Arabel and her brothers, Mr Browning and Sarianna.
But again, the holiday was not a success: Havre was a hideous commercial
city, they longed for the sun and beauty of Florence, and were glad indeed to
return to the comforts of Casa Guidi. They did not stay long, however; the
last winter had been very cold, and this year they decided to go to Rome,
which, thanks to Mr Kenyon, they could now well afford.

The change suited Browning. Elizabeth was better, though with little energy
– gone were the days of six-mile donkey rides – and at last he was able to leave
her in the evenings to take part in the social life of the cosmopolitan city. And

now Elizabeth in her turn was worried: worried by his restlessness, his inability to sit down and write, his gaiety, which she felt was not altogether genuine, but assumed to conceal his mortification, a gesture of contempt for a public that failed to appreciate his poetry. As she wrote to Sarianna:

Robert has made his third bust copied from the antique. He breaks them all up as they are finished – it's only matter of education. When the power of execution is achieved, he will try at something original. Then reading hurts him; so long as I have known him he has not been able to read long at a time – he can do it now better than at the beginning. The consequence of which is that an active occupation is salvation to him. . . . He was not inclined to write this winter. The modelling combines body-work and soul-work, and the more tired he has been, and the more his back ached, poor fellow, the more he has exulted and been happy. . . . .

At the same time, his treatment in England affects him, naturally, and for my part I set it down as an infamy of that public. . . .

As a sort of lion, Robert has his range in society – and – for the rest, you should see Chapman's returns! – While, in America he is a power, a writer, a poet – he is read.

There were other occupations for Browning in this momentous year of 1859. The irascible octogenarian Landor, who had so strangely written that he 'strove with none', yet had been expelled both from school and university for violence, had fled from England to escape a libel action and, penniless, sought refuge in Fiesole, overlooking Florence, with the wife and family he had left twenty years before. There he was so unwelcome, so unhappy, that one morning he appeared at Casa Guidi, and Browning, who loved and revered the old man, wrote to his brothers, who agreed to pay for his support for the rest of his life.

This was in the early summer, by which time events in Italy were approaching a climax. Napoleon III had made an arrangement with Cavour to go to the help of Piedmont – for a consideration – if Austria could be enticed into attacking her. When Austria declared war in April, therefore, Napoleon joined the Piedmontese under their king Victor Emmanuel, and won the battles of Magenta and Solferino. But then, instead of driving the Austrians out of Italy as promised, he halted, leaving Venetia in their hands, Lombardy only being united with Piedmont. The small states of the north, however, including Tuscany, expelled their Dukes and declared themselves republics though by the Treaty of Villafranca their old rulers were to be restored. That was in July, and for Elizabeth, fervent admirer of Napoleon and fanatical supporter of Italian unification, the news of the Peace was almost a death-blow. She collapsed, and for weeks Browning nursed her day and night before taking her to Siena to recuperate. He also took Landor, who stayed first with the Storys, then in a cottage that he rented for him.

Meanwhile, the British Government, all-powerful at sea, insisted that the Italian people should be left to settle their own affairs; so the former rulers of Tuscany, Parma, Modena and the Romagna were not restored, and the little republics decided to become part of the Kingdom of Piedmont. This explains Browning's heading of a letter to the young painter Frederic Leighton: 'Kingdom of Piedmont, Siena: Oct. 9, '59.' He apologised for not having answered earlier Leighton's letter of July:

> I was in great trouble at the time about my wife who was seriously ill. As soon as she could bear removal we brought her to a villa here. She slowly recovered and is at last *well* – I believe – but weak still and requiring more attention than usual. We shall be obliged to return to Rome for the winter – not choosing to risk losing what we have regained with some difficulty. . . .
> The Storys have passed the summer in the villa opposite, – and no less a lion than dear old Landor is in a house a few steps off. I take care of him – his amiable family having clawed him a little too sharply.

They were returning to Florence on the following day, he added, where they would probably stay for a month. They took Landor with them, and Browning saw him comfortably settled in the home of Wilson and her Italian husband near the Casa Guidi. 'He pays four pounds ten (English) the month,' Elizabeth wrote to Sarianna. 'Wilson has thirty pounds a year to look after him – which sounds a good deal, but it is a difficult position. He has excellent, generous, affectionate impulses– but the impulses of the tiger, every now and then.'

In November they returned to Rome, – and Charles Darwin published his *Origin of Species*.

Elizabeth was better, well enough, at least, to prepare her *Poems before Congress* for publication, but there was one thing, in addition to her health and hero-worship of Napoleon, that worried Browning: her continued addiction to spiritualism. The egregious Daniel Home had haunted Florence, and now another American addict, a Mrs Eckley, had attached herself to Elizabeth. In the course of this winter, however, she found that Sophia Eckley was a fraud – English spirits that she conjured were given to writing Americanisms. The discovery, involving the loss of a trusted friend as well as raising doubts about the mysticism in which she so intensely wished to believe, scarcely improved her spirits.

It was probably during this winter of 1859–60 that Browning gave vent to his dislike, hatred is scarcely too strong a word, of spiritualism and mediums, with their attendant ill-effects on his wife's health, and wrote, or partly wrote, 'Mr Sludge, "The Medium" ', for in May 1860 Elizabeth wrote: 'Robert deserves no reproaches, for he has been writing a good deal this winter – working at a long poem which I have not seen a line of, and producing short lyrics which I *have* seen, and may declare worthy of him.' 'Mr Sludge' was scarcely a poem that Browning would wish Elizabeth to see a line of at that time:

> Now, don't, sir! Don't expose me! Just this once!
> This was the first and only time, I'll swear, –
> Look at me, – see, I kneel, – the only time,
> I swear, I ever cheated. . . .

It was from Rome that Elizabeth had written in May, a few days after Garibaldi and his Thousand had sailed from Genoa and landed in Sicily to free it from the rule of the hated Bourbon King of Naples, so that she did not see from Casa Guidi windows Victor Emmanuel's April entry into Florence which she celebrated:

> Flowers, flowers, from the flowery city!
> Such innocent thanks for a deed so pure,
> As, melting away for joy into flowers,
> The nation invites him to enter his Pitti
> And evermore reign in this Florence of ours.
> Be witness, Cavour!
> He'll stand where the reptiles were used to crawl,
> This King of us all.

After the Treaty of Villafranca Cavour had resigned in rage and despair, but in January 1860 he returned. Tuscany and the other northern states – Venetia excepted– were officially incorporated in Piedmont, and Napoleon got his reward – two western provinces of Piedmont: Savoy and Nice. There remained Austrian Venetia, the Papal States, and – most vulnerable – the Bourbon Kingdom of Naples. Cavour did not dare to act openly for fear of offending the Great Powers, but if Garibaldi chose to lead volunteers into Sicily it was no business of his, for the Italian people were to decide their own affairs. So while secretly encouraging Garibaldi he professed ignorance of his expedition, and by June the Neapolitan army had been driven out of Sicily. Cavour could now act openly, and sent volunteer reinforcements to Garibaldi, who crossed to the mainland and in September entered Naples, though he found his way to Rome blocked by the fortress of Capua. Cavour now acted quickly, for he could not afford to let Garibaldi, former defender of the Roman

COURT OF QUEEN'S BENCH, THURSDAY, JULY 1.
(Sittings at Nisi Prius, at Guildhall, before Lord Camp-bell and a Special Jury.)
VON MÜLLER V. BROWNING.

Sir A. Cockburn and another learned gentleman were counsel for the plaintiff; and Mr. Willes for the defendant. Sir A. Cockburn stated that this was an action to recover compensation in damages for a breach of promise of marriage. These cases had more or less romance in them, but he was sorry to say that in this he could not present any such attraction. The plaintiff was a lady of mature age, being 45 years old, and the defendant was 20 years older; but although there was no romance, there was peculiar interest in it on account of the peculiar circumstances of the case. The plaintiff, Mrs. Von Müller, was the widow of an officer in the Austrian service. She was an English lady, whose maiden name was Haynes. Her first marriage was a very unfortunate one; her husband proved to be a spendthrift and a libertine; he got into debt, fell into licentious habits, ruined his family, went into the Spanish service, and ultimately died in that kingdom. Mrs. Meredith, upon her husband's leaving, took refuge with her father and mother, and remained for several years without receiving any tidings of her husband. Rumours arrived from Spain that he had perished there. She had a son and daughter. She met with Captain Von Müller, who was very much struck with her, paid her great attention, and proposed marriage to her; she accepted him conditionally that she should not marry until she got evidence of her husband's death. In the year 1836 she received conclusive evidence of Meredith's death, and then she married Captain Von Müller.

Mr. Willes said he did not mean to cast the smallest imputation on the plaintiff—his client was incapable of it.

Sir A. Cockburn.—The defendant might be incapable of doing so in court, but he had done it again and again in the most cold-blooded manner. The action was brought not only for the purpose of recovering compensation for the breach of promise, but for the wanton and malicious manner in which he had acted in endeavouring to defame her character. Her second marriage was a happy one, but again this lady was doomed to misfortune; for having had another child, she was a second time left a widow. She then again went to live with her father and mother at New Cross. The defendant, who had been for nearly 50 years in the Bank of England, resided near their residence; he was struck with her appearance. He used to pass the house waving his hand, and looking with great earnestness. There was some talk about her going abroad. This, it would seem, was too painful for him, and he sent her an anonymous letter to this effect:—" I hope you will forgive the question, as you are the last person I would give offence to. May I ask, is it true that you are going to quit England? I do not ask from motives of idle curiosity. Need I mention my name? December, 1850." Some amusement was afforded by this letter; but one lady who was in the house had no doubt from whom the letter had come. In a short time the defendant met her in the street, and accosted her, asked leave to accompany her home, and declared his intentions. The plaintiff shortly afterwards went to reside at Upton, and the defendant then commenced a correspondence with her. At first the letters began with "My dear Mrs. Von Müller," but they soon grew warmer. The learned counsel then read upwards of 50 letters which were written by the defendant to the plaintiff; most of them commenced with "My dearest, dearest, dearest, dearest, dearest, dearest much-loved Minny;" they were couched in terms of the greatest warmth, and professed the most intense love of the writer for the lady whom he was addressing. Sometimes there was introduced a considerable essay upon theological subjects, then they would refer in terms of doubt of the propriety of marrying her, in consequence of the statement the plaintiff had made to him regarding the history of her former life, and particularly as to her second marriage, charging her with having been guilty of crime or gross error; but the letters following these would express the greatest regret, and would contain the most abject apologies, even upon his knees, for having written such letters, and assuring her that the hateful subject should never be mentioned again, and that the whole should be confined to his own breast. All these letters proved the defendant to be a man of education and considerable literary attainments. The defendant had returned two or three of the plaintiff's letters, which were evidently written by a very sensible woman. At last the defendant went to his son at Paris, and on the 1st of November a letter was received from the defendant's son, stating that his father had informed him of the manner in which she had annoyed him, and of the persecution he had undergone for some time. The plaintiff wrote a letter in answer, expressing her extreme surprise. Upon this the defendant wrote to her, beginning his letter with "Mrs. Von Müller," and in that letter he gave as a reason for breaking off the match her misconduct from the time she was a girl, "Has not your whole career, from your running away from school to your settling at New Cross, been one continued series of everything but respectable? I believe that when you married your second husband you knew your first husband was alive." The learned counsel then charged the defendant with having been guilty of the

Lord Campbell then summed up.—It seemed to him that this was not a case where the damages should be so large as some that came before the Court, nor by any means so small as to mark any opinion of theirs that the plaintiff had misconducted herself. He did not discover that this lady had held out any lure to this old gentleman; his folly was his own folly. He was smitten with her charms, became attached to her, and asked her to marry him, which she had consented to do. He was a clerk in the Bank, living in a very creditable manner, and was evidently a man of great intellectual powers and of considerable attainments. The plaintiff had been disappointed in her expectations, and was entitled to damages. He agreed with Sir A. Cockburn that if this old gentleman, thinking better of the matter, had come to the opinion that at his advanced period of life, and with his son and daughter, it would be more prudent and expedient not to enter into a fresh matrimonial contract—if he had made a representation upon this subject to the lady—he might have been blamed to a certain degree, but very little to that which it seemed to him he was now to answer. But how had he conducted himself? He must say in a most cowardly manner. He had written the letter of November, wherein he made the imputation against the plaintiff. It appeared to him a very gross case. Exemplary damages the law did not recognize; damages should only be a compensation for injury sustained.

The Jury wished to know what salary the defendant received.

A clerk in the Bank stated that it was about 320l. a year.

The Jury then retired, and in a short time returned into court and gave a verdict for the plaintiff—Damages, 800l.

11. *The Times*, 2 July 1852, and photograph of Browning's father in 1861. *Victoria & Albert Museum.*

RIGHT LEG IN THE BOOT AT LAST.

12. From *Punch* 17 November 1860: Garibaldi presents Victor
Emmanuel with southern Italy. *Reproduced by permission of* Punch.

Republic, overrun central as well as southern Italy. With the consent of Napoleon, therefore, he sent troops from the north to occupy the Papal States, leaving only a small area round Rome for the Pope to rule. On 26 October 1860 Garibaldi met Victor Emmanuel in Naples, and on 8 November handed over the Kingdom of Naples to the first King of Italy.

It was in June, while Garibaldi was driving the Neapolitan troops out of Sicily, that Browning found and bought for a lira from a Florentine stall the old yellow book that was to become the source of *The Ring and the Book:*

> That memorable day,
> (June was the month, Lorenzo named the Square). . . .
> Still read I on, from written title-page
> To written index, on, through street and street,
> At the Strozzi, at the Pillar, at the Bridge;
> Till, by the time I stood at home again
> In Casa Guidi by Felice Church,
> Under the doorway where the black begins
> With the first stone-slab of the staircase cold,
> I had mastered the contents.

Soon afterwards they went to Siena for the summer, where Elizabeth waited anxiously for news of Henrietta who was desperately ill. 'Poor Robert's scheme for me of perfect repose has scarcely been carried out,' she wrote; and not long after their arrival in Rome came the news of her death. Mrs Jameson's death earlier in the year had been a sad loss, but Henrietta's was a blow which, Browning always maintained, hastened her own end. There is a photograph taken in Rome at about this time, showing her seated with head bent, as always, towards the right, her thick dark hair falling beside her face like a spaniel's ears, but leaving exposed the broad brow of her genius. She looks frail but not unhappy, for she is holding the hand of eleven-year-old Pen standing beside her, with hair almost as long as hers, and fantastically dressed and embroidered like a girl in blouse-like tunic and skirt-length trousers. The companion photograph is of Browning himself, his long crumpled jacket making him look even shorter than his modest Victorian 5 feet 8 inches. A year earlier he had shaved off his beard, to the horror of Elizabeth who insisted that he should let it grow again, which (with the addition of moustache) he did; and now she wrote: 'You will think Robert looking very well when you see him; indeed you may judge by the photographs meanwhile. You know, Sarianna, how I used to forbid the moustache. I insisted as long as I could, but all artists were against me. . . . As to the moony whiteness of the beard, it is beautiful, *I* think, but then I think him all beautiful, and always.'

He had taken his yellow Book to Rome in the hope of discovering more about the story that it told:

> I took my book to Rome first, tried truth's power
> On likely people. 'Have you met such names?
> Is a tradition extant of such facts?
> Your law-courts stand, your records frown a-row:
> What if I rove and rummage?' 'Why, you'll waste
> Your pains and end as wise as you began!'
> Everyone snickered: 'names and facts thus old
> Are newer much than Europe news we find
> Down in today's *Diario*. Records, quotha?
> Why, the French burned them. . . .'

There were few foreigners in Rome in the winter of 1860 after the events of that memorable year, and the tragedy that now began on the other side of the Atlantic scarcely encouraged an influx of American visitors. On 4 March 1861 Abraham Lincoln was inaugurated President of the United States, and a month later the Civil War began. But Browning was more concerned about Elizabeth than about Risorgimento, Civil War and a seventeenth-century murder story. She was very ill, but at the beginning of June he managed to get her back to Florence and Casa Guidi, where almost the first news that greeted her was the death of Cavour. On the following day, 7 June, she wrote to Sarianna: 'We come home into a cloud here. I can scarcely command voice or hand to name *Cavour*. That great soul which meditated and made Italy has gone to the diviner Country. . . . A hundred Garibaldis for such a man!'

It was the final blow, for though she appeared to recover a little, early in the morning of 29 June she died smilingly in Robert's arms.

III. LONDON 1861-1889

8. 'Dramatis Personae'
1861–64

IT was the end of a fifteen-years' idyll. On 28 June 1846 Robert had written from New Cross to Elizabeth in Wimpole Street: 'the wind took my thoughts away as it always does, and I saw you again as I used to see, *before* I knew you, so very substanceless, faint, unreal.' On the following day, 29 June, he had visited her and they had discussed the merits of Salerno as a place to live when they were married. It had proved to be Florence – where now, on 29 June 1861, 'substanceless, faint, unreal'. . . . . He was overcome by grief and by memories, but fortunately Isa Blagden was at hand to look after Pen while as best he could he saw to Elizabeth's burial and business affairs. Yet he was not 'prostrated', as he told Frederic Leighton, who designed her monument: 'I have enough to do for the boy and myself in carrying out her wishes.' It was true that Elizabeth had been an inspiration, and so much more than an inspiration, but she had also been something of a burden limiting his activities, as she had warned him, so many years ago, that she might be, and towards the end had told Sarianna 'I am only good for a drag chain.' It may have been, therefore, with mixed feelings of near despair, of unreality, and something approaching relief that he left Florence in July, never to return. He was just forty-nine.

Isa Blagden accompanied him and Pen to Paris, where she left them with old Mr Browning and Sarianna, with whom they went for a holiday near Dinard before moving to London. Browning wished to make a complete break, his new life to resemble as little as possible that in Italy, and instead of buying or renting a house and furnishing it with his treasures from Casa Guidi, he took furnished lodgings near Paddington Station. Not that he was interested in trains, though Pen probably was, but his rooms in Chichester Road were near Elizabeth's sister Arabel, whom he constantly visited.

There was work for the winter in plenty: preparing Elizabeth's *Last Poems* for publication, work that must at times have been near heart-breaking: 'What's the best thing in the world? . . . Love, where, *so*, you're loved again.'

And to 'The North to the South' he added the note, 'The Last Poem. Rome, May, 1861.' His work was finished in February 1862, when he wrote a dedication 'To Grateful Florence.'

He had just heard of the death of Rossetti's wife. 'Poor, dear fellow!' he wrote to Isa. 'Another melancholy thing – ' and he told sad stories of the desperate illnesses of two more women. 'So one lives! And so would *not* I live, if this life were all, – no indeed!'[11] His depression throughout the year 1862 is reflected in further letters to his 'best woman friend', written every month on the 19th to commemorate the day of his flight with Elizabeth. 'I shall go *nowhere* . . . the presence of Her is now habitual to me.' And Florence: 'I have such yearnings to be there!' 'Oh me – to find myself there . . . ten minutes *home*. I think I should fairly end it all on the spot.'

Yet for Elizabeth's sake he had to go on, and for Pen's sake to live in London, at least for some years. 'You know I have her dearest wishes and interests to attend to *at once*,' he had written to Fanny Haworth, 'her child to care for, educate, establish properly.' Yet his first move in caring for her child, now in his thirteenth year, would have made Elizabeth weep; for there were three things about which they had disagreed: spiritualism, Napoleon III, and Pen's appearance, and '*at once*', within a few days of her death, the little long-haired girlish-looking Italian in silks and satins was transformed into a short-haired English boy in Victorian woollens, a metamorphosis that must have been a traumatic experience for this spoiled child of Tuscany. Elizabeth, however, would have approved, at least in part, of her husband's plan for his education: he was not to go away to school, but he himself with the aid of a tutor would give him an English, that is, Latin and Greek, education at home, and prepare him for the university. But a lodging cluttered with Victorian furniture was no place in which to bring up the boy, so in the summer he sent for his Casa Guidi treasures and moved into the house that he was to occupy for the next 25 years, 19 Warwick Crescent, facing a small lake formed by the junction of two canals, a house even nearer Paddington Station, and almost next door to Arabel Barrett. Another near neighbour in whom he might have been interested was a young man from Dorset who had just arrived, one Thomas Hardy, more interested in poetry than in his profession of architect.

So Browning, who had left Regency London as a youngish man of 34, returned and settled at the age of 50 into a rapidly expanding Victorian London of red-brick offices, warehouses, railway stations, villas and churches, beneath which the first underground trains were beginning to rumble. The Prince Consort had died soon after Elizabeth, and work was soon to begin on the

Albert Memorial, incidentally commemorating therefore the time of Browning's return, as the progress of its erection may be said to have recorded his rising reputation. For happily, his return coincided with the so-long delayed appreciation of his work. This was partly owing to his friends John Forster and Barry Cornwall, whose *Selections from the Poetical Works of Robert Browning* appeared at the beginning of 1863, when reviews were generally, if cautiously, favourable. It is true that some critics still grumbled about obscurity, and others complained, as Kingsley had done, that he lived in Italy, and even wrote about Italy, which he obviously preferred to his native country, a preference that was 'almost repulsive' to true-born Englishmen. Yet others wrote appreciatively of his passion for Italian freedom, maintaining that it was high time to do justice to Browning, to his dramatic skill, his mastery of the passions, originality, humour; he was not a poet for the nursery, but 'brusque, quaint, rugged, intricately ingenious, ironical – he perplexes the dull and startles the timid.' Browning himself had prepared a three-volume collected edition of his work which came out in 1863, and his publishers were so delighted with its success that they postponed publication of the new poems that he had submitted, so giving him time to add a few more.

Instead of taking Elizabeth to Siena or the Baths of Lucca for the summer, he had now begun to take Pen for a holiday with his father and sister on the coast of Brittany, and in 1862 and 1863 spent some two months at Ste Marie, near Pornic, a hamlet 'Just where the sea and the Loire unite:' a 'little church, a field, a few houses, and the sea.' Here he probably wrote the greater part of 'James Lee's Wife', the bleak monologue of a woman on the coast of Brittany, whose marriage has failed. Written in a mood of depression, it is the reverse of Elizabeth's and his own trimphant love, and may have been inspired by Meredith's just published sonnet sequence 'Modern Love' which he greatly admired. But it is not Browning at this best; although he identified himself with the woman, and there is genuine pathos in her reverie, her often staccato utterance lent itself to parody, which Swinburne, as yet no admirer of Browning's work, took advantage of in 'John Jones's Wife', in section IV of which, 'Up the Spout', he wrote:

> Hi! Just you drop that! Stop, I say!
> Shirk work, think slink off, twist friend's wrist?
> Where that spined sand's lined band's the bay –
> Lined blind with true sea's blue, as due –
> Promising – not to pay?

But the jingling internal rhyme is more characteristic of 'Dis aliter Visum', probably another product of Pornic. Again the speaker is a woman, who tells a writer of 'verse and worse' that by not marrying her ten years before he has ruined two lives, 'nay four':

> For Stephanie sprained last night her wrist,
> Ankle or something. 'Pooh,' cry you?
> At any rate she danced, all say,
> Vilely; her vogue has had its day.
> Here comes my husband from his whist.

Neither of these poems, sometimes speech within speech within speech, makes easy reading, but 'Gold Hair' is a straightforward story of Pornic, of a girl who, before her death and burial, hid gold coins in her golden hair, presumably to buy her way into heaven. But the story, 'this horrible verse', is merely the text and pretext for a short sermon that begins, not very lucidly:

> Evil or good may be better or worse
> In the human heart, but the mixture of each
> Is a marvel and a curse.

Browning had returned to England at a time of great religious controversy. Darwin's *Origin of Species* (1859) had led to the famous British Association debate of 1860, when Bishop Wilberforce assured Thomas Huxley that rock-pigeons were what rock-pigeons had always been, and asked him whether it was from his grandfather or his grandmother that he claimed descent from a monkey; and Wilberforce, no scientist, was in his turn assured that, as a grand-parent, a miserable ape was preferable to a bishop who ridiculed scientific discussion. Then, in the following year, John Colenso, Bishop of Natal, published a *Commentary* denying the doctrine of eternal punishment, and seven authors in England, one of whom was Benjamin Jowett, future Master of Balliol College, published *Essays and Reviews*, demanding freedom of inquiry into religious matters. Denounced by the irrepressible Wilberforce, the book was officially condemned by the Church, and 11,000 clergymen affirmed their belief in the inspiration of the Bible and eternal punishment. This explains the penultimate verse of 'Gold Hair':

> The candid incline to surmise of late
> That the Christian faith proves false, I find;

though not the strangely fundamentalist lines of the conclusion:

> 'Tis the faith that launched point-blank her dart
> At the head of a lie – taught Original Sin,
> The Corruption of Man's Heart.

But this may well be a defiant exposition of Elizabeth's beliefs, as *Christmas Eve and Easter Day* had been of those of another dead woman, his mother. And Jowett was to become one of Browning's great friends.

Oddly enough, another friendship that began at this period, 1863, was with a niece of Darwin, Julia Wedgwood who, Darwin said, understood his book perfectly. A member of a distinguished family descended from the eighteenth-century potter Josiah Wedgwood and the scientist Erasmus Darwin, she was an intelligent unmarried woman of 30 in search of an intelligent man. Isolated by deafness as Elizabeth had been isolated by physical weakness, she wrote to Browning whose work she admired, and Browning, who spoke loudly, responded, beginning to call at her home in Cumberland Place much as he had called on Elizabeth in Wimpole Street twenty years before. But there, apart from the letter-writing,[12] the resemblance ended, for Julia had little sense of humour, was much given to morbidity, and constantly harped on Browning's age (though it is true that his contemporary Thackeray had just died, like Shakespeare aged 52): 'you must expect to be visited by the infirmities of advancing life'; 'I want to make the most of your declining years'; 'how I hope you may not survive your son. . . . And yet I daresay it would not be so terrible to you, remembering whom he would join. . . . I am going to pay a visit to another aged man!' The friendship, therefore, was entirely platonic, yet Browning found it stimulating at this critical period of his recovery, 1863–64, and it is just possible that he now wrote another dramatic monologue, 'Caliban upon Setebos', inspired by *The Origin of Species*, the consequent renewal of interest in natural theology, and by Shakespeare's *Tempest*. But much more probably he had written it shortly before Elizabeth's death, soon after finishing 'Mr Sludge'. The much heralded tercentenary of Shakespeare's birth was approaching, and while writing 'Sludge' in 1860 Browning was obviously re-reading the plays, for his poem is full of phrases from *Hamlet* – 'the top o' your bent', 'very like a whale' – and if he read chronologically, 'Caliban' would follow 'Sludge' as *The Tempest* followed *Hamlet*. From *The Tempest*, then, he took the ape-man Caliban, who tries to imagine his 'dam's God, Setebos', who turns out to be very like Caliban himself:

> Were this no pleasure, lying on the thyme,
> Drinking the mash, with brain become alive,
> Making and marring clay at will? So He.

This, of course, is the poem's moral: that God is beyond man's reason, beyond his natural theology, which can only create a god in his own image, whether

135

prehistoric or Victorian, as Browning made clear in his prefixed quotation from Psalm 50: 'Thou thoughtest that I was altogether such a one as thyself.' (He did not add the next verse, which again is very like Caliban: 'Now consider this, ye that forget God, lest I tear you in pieces.') But 'Caliban' is an entertaining satire, full of poetry and memories of Camberwell and New Cross, of the efts, bees, ants and spiders of their gardens.

The Shakespeare Tercentenary celebrations began on 23 April 1864, and after allowing time for the excitement and interest to subside, Chapman and Hall published *Dramatis Personae* at the end of May. It was the first volume of new poems by Browning since *Men and Women* of 1855, which it resembled in being mainly a number of monologues by men and women. But there were important differences. Although the time and place of four of the poems are widespread as ever – 'A Death in the Desert' is first-century Middle-East, 'Rabbi Ben Ezra' somewhere in twelfth-century Europe, 'Abt Vogler' late eighteenth-century Germany, 'Caliban' perhaps prehistoric Patagonia – the other 14 are modern: three about Pornic, one about Paris, and the scene of the longest, 'Mr Sludge', is Boston, not Lincolnshire but Massachusetts. There is no poem about Renaissance painting, no poem about Italy. Then, by no means all the poems are truly dramatic in the sense that a character other than Browning speaks, though some of the short ones are: elegiac or humorous lyrical monolgues that Elizabeth treasured. One is the 20-line 'May and Death' written some ten years before to commemorate the death of his friend and cousin James Silverthorne, another, 'Confessions', the brief tragi-comedy of an unrepentant man dying among his physic bottles – Browning at his monosyllabic best:

> Alas,
> We loved, sir – used to meet:
> How sad and bad and mad it was –
> But then, how it was sweet!

Another difference between *Dramatis Personae* and *Men and Women* is its reflection of the difference between the world of 1864 and 1855. In 1863 *The Origin of Species* was in its third edition, Huxley published *Man's Place in Nature* and Joseph Renan *La Vie de Jésus* in which he denied the miracles and portrayed Jesus as merely an altruistic young preacher. It was no longer true that, as Browning had assured Ruskin, 'the people hate to be taught.' The critics now assured them that Shakespeare was as great a teacher as he was a dramatist, that in his plays 'we have Thought, History, Exposition, Philosophy, all within the round of the poet.' The people wanted to be taught, or at least assured that their old beliefs were true: belief in the Bible and immortality, belief that they were made in the image of God, not in the image of the ape. By the end of the year, *Dramatis Personae* had gone into a second edition, the first time such a thing had happened to one of Browning's publications.

For in the later poems, written after Elizabeth's death, Browning had set out deliberately, not incidentally, to teach, to reassure, not only others but himself, so that, despite the title, many of the main characters are not really dramatis personae, but Browning himself in a series of disguises. He had forgotten, or discarded, his former axiom, that all the characters in his poems were dramatic. Thus, 'A Death in the Desert' is a defence of the Gospel of St John, the authenticity of which Renan denied. It begins something in the manner of 'The Epistle of Karshish', that is, delightfully, as even the young atheist Swinburne admitted, but added that the poem was soon 'swamped in controversial shallows, and the finer features effaced under a mask of indurate theological mud.' Few would agree; but it is true that the dying evangelist has a long story to tell, for he is the only survivor of those who knew Jesus. In the old days 'men believed ... men believed,' but then came doubters, though

'I never thought to call down fire on such,
Or, as in wonderful and early days,
Pick up the scorpion, tread the serpent dumb.'

'Love' is the key-word, and finally he asseverates his own belief: 'I say ... I say':

'I say, the acknowledgement of God in Christ
Accepted by thy reason, solves for thee
All questions in the earth and out of it.'

He dies, and the poem ends as quietly and dramatically as it had begun.

So much for Renan. But there were other doubters to be dealt with, and better known than 'A Death in the Desert' is Browning's robust declaration of faith through the mouth of the medieval Jewish scholar Ben Ezra. Indeed, the reader could scarcely forget the rhyming chiming lines that carry him along so easily, so confidently, without any confusing excursions into unfamiliar territory. It was Browning's reply to Edward FitzGerald's *Omar Khayyám* and its melancholy philosophy:

Then to this earthen Bowl did I adjourn
My Lip the secret Well of Life to learn:
    And Lip to Lip it murmur'd – 'While you live
Drink! – for once dead you never shall return.'

Not so cries Ezra-Browning to his reader:

Thou, to whom fools propund,
When the wine makes its round,
'Since life fleets, all is change; the Past gone, seize
to-day!'
Fool! All that is, at all,
Lasts ever, past recall;
Earth changes, but thy soul and God stand sure.

There is no argument, merely assertion: 'Grow old along with me! / The best is yet to be.' Happily, it was to prove true, or almost true, for the fifty-year-old Browning, even with his memories of Italy with Elizabeth, about whom he was to have something more to say to the shade of FitzGerald.

Even when he turned to his beloved music, it was no longer of Galuppi playing toccatas at the clavichord, of perishsed men and dear dead women that he thought, but of Abt Vogler at his organ building invisible palaces to God, and moralising on the value of discord and suffering:

Why rushed the discords in but that harmony should be prized?
Sorrow is hard to bear, and doubt is slow to clear,
Each sufferer says his say, his scheme of the weal and woe:
But God has a few of us whom he whispers in the ear;
The rest may reason and welcome: 'tis we musicians know.

Browning himself was a musician, a composer in a modest way as well as a performer, and he knew. But Mr Sludge was no musician.

'Mr Sludge, "The Medium" ', much the longest poem in the book, was probably the 'long poem' that Elizabeth knew Browning was writing in the spring of 1860, though she was never to see it. David Sludge, of course, was inspired – if that is the right word – by Daniel Home, the American medium who had, Browning thought, so grossly deceived his wife, and in the poem he is shown confessing to his patron Hiram H. Horsefall, who has discovered his fraud. But he exacts his price: a free ticket to England for a full account of his tricks. Gathering confidence, he tells Horsefall that he and others like him are really to blame, for they encouraged him to take step after step in their search for proof of their immortality, from spirits merely tapping tables to spirits writing, and finally speaking: Caesar, Franklin, Beethoven, Shakespeare, Lady Jane Grey and Hiram's sainted mother. Yet,

As for religion – why, I served it, sir!
I'll stick to that! With my *phenomena*
I laid the atheist sprawling on his back. . . .
Since Samuel's ghost appeared to Saul, of course
My brother's spirit may appear to me.

So Sludge is allowed to defend himself, and he makes a good case, for Browning was deeply interested in the man's motives, and treated him with much the same humour as Chaucer had treated his Pardoner. Yet the poem finishes in truly Browningesque manner when Sludge has reached the safety of his bedroom:

> R-r-r, you brute-beast and blackguard. Cowardly scamp! . . .
> You throttled your sainted mother, that old hag. . . .
> To get this house of hers.

'Mr Sludge' would have delighted Landor had he read it, but he died a few weeks after its publication.

Browning wrote an 'Epilogue' to *Dramatis Personae*, summarising his creed in 1864, but the real key to the poems lies in 'Prospice' ('Look Forwards'), almost a prologue, written when he had almost recovered from the shock of Elizabeth's death. It reads like a man desperately singing to keep up his spirits, beating his breast and boasting, shouting, that he is not afraid of death but, ever a fighter like the heroes of old, will meet the Arch Fear open-eyed, face to face, until the inevitable 'black minute's at end' – and then, quietly, gently, and all the more moving after the introductory bombast:

> Then a light, then thy breast,
> O thou soul of my soul! I shall clasp thee again,
> And with God be the rest!

There are, then, three distinct periods represented in *Dramatis Personae*. First: 'Sludge', 'Caliban', and a number of dramatic lyrics such as 'Confessions', written before Elizabeth's death, half-humorous and wholly dramatic in the manner of *Men and Women*. Then, the bleak Pornic poems such as 'James Lee's Wife', written in the period of depression after her death. Finally, the religious poems introduced by 'Prospice': 'A Death in the Desert', 'Rabbi Ben Ezra', 'Abt Vogler', humourless didactic poems more in the mood of *Christmas Eve and Easter Day*, written after the death of his mother, and, indeed, summarised in the 'Epilogue'. *Easter Day* had been followed by *Men and Women*; *Dramatis Personae* was to be followed by *The Ring and the Book*.

More immediately came the applause, the acclaim, when for the first time critics welcomed with few reservations a volume by Browning. It is true that *The Times*, 'The Thunderer', found 'James Lee' a puzzle, but congratulated the author on his leaving Italy for his native country, and learning to think and feel as an Englishman should. The reception of 'Caliban' was mixed: only a great dramatic poet could have written it, one critic averred, but others found the subject 'disagreeable', like 'Sludge', and the greatest praise was reserved for the didactic poems. 'Rabbi Ben Ezra' was splendid, but 'A Death in the Desert' even better, 'the finest poem in the book'. More generally: Mr Browning was 'in the foremost rank of modern poets', 'the most original of contemporary poets', 'the Michael Angelo of poets'; 'of the living masters of English poetry, Robert Browning gives us the greatest measure of delight.' And again: 'massive and weighty thoughts'; 'those poems in which Mr Browning deals with historical religious subjects are his masterpieces . . . the knowledge which it is the business of Mr Browning, and all great modern poets, to teach.'

To teach! Fortunately Browning was even more interested in human nature than in teaching. But he had arrived. No longer was he merely the husband, or widower, of Elizabeth Barrett, merely 'the author of *Paracelsus*', but the author of *Dramatis Personae*, a poet comparable to, though very different from, the Laureate Tennyson, at least among the more literate, more intelligent members of the younger generation.

9. 'The Ring and the Book'

1864–69

ON 2 August 1864 Browning wrote to Julia Wedgwood: 'Goodbye, dearest friend, I go tomorrow, stay, as I very likely have told you, some two months.' Then on 19 September to Isa Blagden from Biarritz at the foot of the Western Pyrenees: 'I stayed a month at green pleasant little Cambo, and then came here.' He and Pen had been joined by his father and Sarianna, and Pen's 'red cheeks look as they should. For me, I have got on by having a great read at Euripides – the one book I brought with me, besides attending to my own matters, my new poem that is about to be; and of which the whole is pretty well in my head – the Roman murder story you know.' He had visited the Pas de Roland, and it was in that mountain gorge, according to W. G. Rossetti, that he conceived the full plan of *The Ring and the Book*.

On his return at the beginning of October he began to write, working so steadily and quickly every morning that he was soon able to tell Isa and Julia that he expected to finish the twelve Books in little more than six months. On 19 October he wrote to Leighton in Rome to ask him to have a look at the interior of the church of St Lorenzo in the Corso – of course he knew the Guido Reni 'Crucifixion' over the altar – so that he could remind him of unimportant detail on his return. Leighton did so, and at the beginning of Book 2 Browning wrote:

> The beggarly transept with its bit of apse. . . .
> the little marble balustrade. . . .
> the wooden work
> Painted like porphyry to deceive the eye.

Nevertheless, the poem began to take longer than anticipated, though at the beginning of November 1865, after a year's work, Browning was able to tell Allingham that he had written 15,000 lines, that is, about eight of the twelve Books.

There had been interruptions. He had prepared for publication a selection of Elizabeth's poems, for which he wrote a prefatory note. Pen's education had to be supervised, and in the summer he took the boy to Pornic to read Virgil. But Pen, now sixteen with 'dreadfully incipient moustachios', was probably more interested in the daughters and maidservant of the Mayor in whose house they lodged than in the Queen of Carthage. Then, there had been an unexpected incident that must have upset Browning. On 1 March Julia Wedgwood had written to ask him not to call on her again: 'I have reason to know that my pleasure in your company has had an interpretation put upon it that I ought not to allow. . . . You have only accepted a position into which I invited you – remember I invited you.' She, therefore, was in a position to forbid further meetings, and she hoped he would understand. He wrote to say that the decision was hers, but added mischievously, 'two persons who suddenly unclasp arms and start off in opposite directions look terribly intimate. . . . God bless you, my dearest friend.'

More important to the world as a whole than Pen's education and a spinster's qualms were two events of international significance. On the evening of 14 April President Lincoln was shot by a fanatic while watching a play in a Washington theatre, and died early on the following morning. But he died at the moment of triumph; the Civil War was over and slavery abolished in the southern states, which had been prevented from breaking away to form another republic. The United States of America was on the way to becoming the world's greatest power, though for the next half-century that position was to be held by Britain and her Empire. Exactly six months after Lincoln's death came that of the 80-year-old Lord Palmerston, who had been Prime Minister for the last ten years. Young Thomas Hardy was at the funeral service in Westminster Abbey, and wrote to his sister: 'Only fancy, Ld. P. has been connected with the govt. off and on for the last 60 years, and that he was contemporaneous with Pitt, Fox, Sheridan, Burke, etc. I mean to say his life overlapped theirs so to speak.' It was true, though to Browning the period of Pitt did not seem as remote as it did to the future author of *The Dynasts*, nearly thirty years younger than he. Yet Palmerston had been Secretary-at-War before he was born, and the old statesman's death was prologue to another era, that of Disraeli and Gladstone and Imperial grandeur.

It was also the beginning of another era for Browning, or, in a sense, a return to, a continuation of, that of twenty years earlier, before he met Elizabeth. Now a literary lion, the author of *Dramatis Personae* had re-entered society, where his charm, conviviality and exuberant talk made him much sought after. 'I dine with Lady Wm Russell tonight,' he wrote to Isa, '& then go to Lady Salisbury's – tomorrow Sartoris, – next day, Lady Palmerston's

&c &c . . . dining out in a way that looks absurd enough: at last – my head began to turn in an ominous way, one morning.' And now there was no Elizabeth to recommend hot foot-baths, riding, tobacco, even a glass of wine as remedies. No wonder 'The Roman Murder Story' made little progress in 1866. There were other reasons for delay, however. In June he received a telegram from Sarianna, informing him that their father was desperately ill. He hurried to Paris where he was able to spend a day with the old man, nearly 85, before he died, so happily that he wondered why his children were so affected by his going. 'He was worthy of being Ba's father,' Browning wrote simply. The loss meant even more to Sarianna, who had spent the 17 years since their mother's death looking after him, and now she moved to London to keep house for her brother.

Mr Browning died in the middle of the Seven Weeks' War in which Prussia defeated Austria, and in return for her help rewarded Italy with her long-lost province of Venetia. It was prelude to a greater and more ominous war that was to follow four years later.

Meanwhile, for Browning there was much ado about Oxford. He had recently met Benjamin Jowett, the great classical scholar and tutor of Balliol College, who had written of him: 'I had no idea that there was a perfectly sensible poet in the world, entirely free from enmity, jealousy, or any other littleness, and thinking no more of himself than if he were an ordinary man. His great energy is very remarkable, and his determination to make the most of the remainder of his life.' It is a description worth remembering, written by a formidably critical contemporary not given to superlatives. The two men became friends, and it was partly owing to Jowett that Browning's name was put forward as a candidate for the Poetry Professorship on Matthew Arnold's retirement in 1867. But there were difficulties: Browning was not an Oxford man, not even a university man, his nomination was late, and nothing came of the proposal. He was not unduly disappointed; three lectures a year, he said, would have taken as much time as the writing of three tragedies; but he would have accepted for the sake of Pen, who was to spend the next three or four years at the University. For he had decided that Pen must go to Oxford, and to Balliol under Jowett's tuition. However, thanks again to Jowett, other, more welcome, un-onerous honours awaited him. In June he was given an honorary M.A. degree – the first to receive one since Dr Johnson who, anyway, was an Oxford man– and in October he was elected an Honorary Fellow of Balliol, which meant that he would be able to stay in his own rooms in Pen's college.

The trouble was that Pen, though clever, was no dedicated scholar. In 1866, unable to face Pornic again, with its memories of their father, Browning and Sarianna had taken him to Croisic, just north of the mouth of the Loire, where he had spent his time swimming and shooting – 'alas!' In October, however, they were back in Warwick Crescent, where Browning worked at his poem in the intervals of coaching Pen in Latin and Greek, though at the beginning of 1867 he had to admit that the boy was more interested in boating, shooting and breech-loaders than in serious scholarship: 'he is a good fellow all the same, and may wake up ambitious one day.' The reason for this concentrated classical coaching was Jowett's suggestion that Pen should go to stay with him in Balliol so that he could give him an unofficial test. He got on very well with the undergraduates he met there, but Jowett had to report that though his Latin was up to Balliol standard his Greek was far behind. Yet in the summer, at Croisic again, the pattern of the previous year was repeated: shooting and swimming, and Browning himself, always fond of bathing, now became an enthusiastic long-distance swimmer. While Pen was shooting, however, he wrote the delightful ballad-like 'Hervé Riel', celebrating the forgotten hero of Croisic who in 1692 saved the French fleet from destruction by piloting it safely into harbour and, as a reward, asked for a day's holiday to go to see his wife. 'The Two Poets of Croisic', also inspired by these holidays, was written ten years later.

Instead of matriculating that autumn, 1867, Pen went to Oxford to be coached. He was there at the beginning of the following year, when Browning went to visit his 'brother Dons', shortly before his new publishers, Smith, Elder, issued a six-volume edition of 'The Poetical Works of Robert Browning, M.A., Honorary Fellow of Balliol College, Oxford.' But Pen was still not good enough for Balliol, and while Browning and Sarianna went to Audierne to see the prehistoric remains of Carnac and Finisterre, he went with Jowett and a reading party to Scotland. Yet it was no good, and in January 1869, then nearly twenty, he was accepted by Christ Church, where, wrote Browning, 'he is enjoying himself extremely.'

We can follow the major – and minor and trivial – events in Browning's life during these critical years of anxiety about Pen and of writing *The Ring and the Book*, for his monthly letters to Isa Blagden are almost an autobiography. Thus, at one dinner-party he met, and liked, John Bright who talked radicalism to a neighbouring duke; at another the Liberal leaders Lord John Russell and Gladstone, 'looking radiant', at the time of the passing of the Reform Bill of 1867, which gave the vote to far more men – not of course women, not Sarianna, for example. Tennyson he often met, and Matthew Arnold, whom he liked as much as his poems. Then, there was the actor with whom he had quarrelled more than twenty years before, William Macready, 'so old & changed, so uninterested in his old life! His wife is a Plymouth Sister, – never entered a theatre in her life. This seems to abolish the whole past existence of such a man.' Yet there was no abolishing his own past, the years with Eliza-beth: 'The general impression of the past is as if it had been pain. I would not live it over again, not one day of it. Yet all that seems my real *life*, – and before and after, nothing at all.' And again, at the beginning of 1868, left in Warwick Crescent without Pen who had been his constant companion for 19 years: 'How my whole soul turns to Italy, words are weak to tell you – how I wish myself there, out of all this ugliness. If I live & do well, it shall be. "Anywhere, anywhere out of this black rainy beastly-streeted London world." I get quite sick of dining-out – refuse whatever invitations I possibly can.' To add to his despondency, six months later he lost another companion, when Arabel, last of the three Barrett sisters, his old friend and neighbour, died, like Elizabeth, in his arms. Even at the end of his enjoyable Audierne holiday he almost dreaded the thought of Warwick Crescent: 'The place will be sad to return to, with no more Arabel, – dear Arabel! I had fancied I might take another house, – but after all, it matters so little.'

That was written on 19 October, and a month later, on 21 November 1868, the first volume of *The Ring and the Book* was published, more than eight years after Browning had bought the Old Yellow Book in Florence on that memorable midsummer day of 1860. Three more volumes followed at monthly intervals, each, like the first, containing three of the twelve Books, so it was not until the end of February 1869 that the complete poem of 21,000 lines was revealed.

The title-page of the Yellow Book was, like 'The Murder of Gonzago' in *Hamlet*, 'writ in choice Italian', (with a Latin postscript) which may be rendered:

An Account
Of the whole Criminal Case
Against
Guido Franceschini, Nobleman
of Arezzo, and his cut-throats,
put to death in Rome the 22nd
February 1698,
The first by beheading, the other
four by hanging.

ROME MURDER CASE
Disputing if and when a Husband
may kill an Audlterous Wife
without incurring the ordinary penalty.

Given such material, an additional pamphlet describing the execution, and Browning's knowledge of Italian, it would appear to be relatively easy to write a blank-verse account of the melodrama; but when it is realised that the Yellow Book gives little but a series of legal arguments, that the speech of the leading characters is never directly reported but has to be inferred or imagined – when this is realised, the wonder of creating nine different interpretations, nine versions and perversions of, nine dramatic monologues on, the same theme will be appreciated.

But first, the story, as objectively as possible. Count Guido Franceschini, a 50-year-old impoverished nobleman of Arezzo, near Florence, marries the 13-year-old humbly-born Pompilia Comparini of Rome for her money, which turns out to be less than he expected. After four unhappy months of insult at Arezzo, Pompilia's putative parents, Violante and Pietro, return to Rome, where Violante confesses that, unknown to Pietro, the girl is really a prostitute's daughter whom she had bought to secure an inheritance left to their child if they had one, and they demand the return of the money. Guido avenges himself on Pompilia who, after some four years' ill-treatment, appeals to the young Canon Giuseppe Caponsacchi to take her back to her home in Rome. They are caught by Guido at an inn at Castelnuovo, arrested, tried and found guilty of adultery. Caponsacchi is relegated for three years, Pompilia confined in a Roman Convent of Convertites, but because of her pregnancy allowed to go home. There she gives birth to a son, and a few days later Guido with four accomplices mortally wound her and kill Violante and Pietro.

The murderers are arrested, tried and found guilty, but Guido, as a priest in minor orders, claims right of appeal to the Pope. But the Pope pronounces him guilty, and Guido and his accomplices are executed. The Court then declares Pompilia innocent and her baby son her lawful heir.

The title 'The Ring and the Book' was as enigmatic as had been the 'Bells and Pomegranates' of twenty years before, and this time Browning began with a detailed explanation. The Book was easily explained: 'Do you see this square old yellow Book, I toss/I' the air? . . . I found this book. . . .' But the significance of the Ring was less obvious: 'Do you see this Ring? 'Tis Rome-work. . . .' He was thinking of a gold ring that he had given Elizabeth, and as the ring had been shaped by the addition of an alloy to the gold ore, so his poem was shaped by the addition of imagination, of poetry, to the inert material of the Yellow Book.

Book 1, therefore, is not a dramatic monologue, but Browning himself as prologue: describing how he found the Book, an outline of its story, how his imagination shaped it – 'Such substance of me interfused the gold' – an outline of the eleven books that follow, and a whispered Websterian description of preparations for the execution:

> slow sweep
> And settle down in silence solidly,
> Crow-wise, the frightful Brotherhood of death.
> Black-hatted and black-hooded huddle they,
> Black rosaries a-dangling from each waist;
> So take they their grim station at the door,
> Torches lit, skull-and-cross-bones banner spread.

Finally, he addressed a few words to the 'British Public, ye who like me not, (God bless you!)', and added a posy to the ring, a dedication of his poem to Elizabeth:

> O lyric Love, half angel and half bird
> And all a wonder and a wild desire, –

a vow never to begin, never to end, a poem without thoughts of her, his inspiration: a prayer that 'What was, again may be.'

The first three monologues are spoken before Guido's trial for murder, before the Court has given judgement, found him guilty. Thus, it is in the church of San Lorenze in Lucina, to which the mutilated bodies of Violante and Pietro have just been carried, that the speaker of Book 2 meets just the man he wishes to meet, cousin of another man who has persuaded him that Guido is the guilty one. He, 'Half-Rome', represents the ordinary Roman citizen, who, crammed with rumour, but with little factual knowledge, is prejudiced in favour of the husband; and a good case he makes for the 'honest man' against the 'child-cheat' and unspeakable Violante, the imagery being appropriately that of angler – bait and cold-blooded creatures: spider, toad, viper, scorpion. At one point, however, he oversteps the mark, when he says that, before Pompilia fled from Arezzo with her paramour Caponsacchi, she drugged Guido and his household, stole their money and jewels and set fire to the house. Subjected to one humiliation after another, the final one being the birth of Pompilia's illegitimate son, 'Guido revenged his own wrong like a gentleman.' He will be justified, and the trial is to follow

only for form's sake. Then, with a characteristic Browningesque twist, the
speaker concludes:

> a matter I commend
> To the notice, during Carnival that's near,
> Of a certain what's-his name and jackanapes
> Somewhat too civil of eves with lute and song
> About a house here, where I keep a wife.
> (You, being his cousin, may go tell him so.)

The representative of 'The Other Half-Rome' in Book 3 is a chivalrous
bachelor whose sympathies are all with Pompilia who, now two days after
the murderous attack, is still miraculously alive. She is innocent, and letters
said to have been written by her, an illiterate girl, are Guido's forgeries; she
had never even spoken to Caponsacchi until the day she appealed to him,
and St George-like he had rescued her. Nor was there any fault in Violante
who, by adopting the child had saved her from being drowned by her
strumpet-mother, and with Pietro had been cheated and maltreated by Guido.
Another character is introduced: the Chaucerian Abate Paolo who persuades
Violante to let his elder brother Guido marry the twelve-year-old Pompilia:

> So – giving now his great flap-hat a gloss
> With flat o' the hand between whiles, soothing now
> The silk from out its creases o'er the calf. . . .
> And somehow the Abate's guardian eye –
> Scintillant, rutilant, fraternal fire, –
> Roving round every way had seized the prize.

But best of all is the speaker's defence of Pompilia's flight when, unknown to
her, she is one month gone with child:

> So when the she-dove breeds, strange yearnings come
> For the unknown shelter by undreamed-of shores,
> And there is born a blood-pulse in her heart
> To fight if needs be, though with flap of wing,
> For the wool-flock or the fur-tuft, though a hawk
> Contest the prize, – wherefore, she knows not yet.

This simile of maternal love is immediately followed by a metaphor of paternal
hate when Guido hears the news:

> Then did the winch o' the winepress of all hate,
> Vanity, disappointment, grudge and greed,
> Take the last turn that screws out pure revenge
> With a bright bubble at the brim beside.

The bubbling labials are heartless here as the gutturals (always so dramatically employed by Browning) are cruel, and a few lines later Violante and Pietro are dead, and Pompilia dying.

A day later, after the 'rabble's babble', a courtier, the 'Tertium Quid' third party of Book 4, tells his aristocratic audience of Excellency this, Highness that, Marquis, Prince and Duke the truth o' the matter that they could so easily decide without a trial. Browning obviously enjoyed writing the snobbish heartlessness of the first part, particularly the description of Violante whose finery in church made her neighbours sigh 'at the load of lace that came to pray', before stealing away to the harlot in her garret to buy the unborn babe – a sin that saved a soul. Then there is Paolo who, twelve years later, takes over his brother Guido's matrimonial affairs, finds Pompilia for him, and prevents his rushing to Pietro to propose a match, for

> 'Priests play with women, maids, wives, mothers – why?
> These play with men and take them off our hands.'

After the marriage comes each party's discovery of the other's cheating. Who is to blame? On the one hand – on the other hand – they say – they also say – but then – and a fine confusion of alternatives ends in:

> The long and the short is, truth seems what I show. . . .
> He is noble, and he may be innocent.
> On the other hand. . . .

But by this time Her Excellency is ready for the gaming-table, Her Highness for bed, and the speaker concludes:

> Both know as much about it, now, at least,
> As all Rome: no particular thanks, I beg!
> (You'll see, I have not so advanced myself,
> After my teaching the two idiots here!)

After the introductory first four Books, the Play itself, as the three surviving characters in the melodrama, *dramatis personae*, give their versions of events to the Court. First Guido Franceschini, recently racked and correspondingly wary, gives a plausible, apparently straightforward account of his virtuous life from boyhood until his present wholly undeserved predicament. Swindled by Violante-Pietro, cuckolded by Pompilia-Caponsacchi whom he might have killed when he found them at the inn had he not respected the law too much to take it into his own hands, and the law had found them guilty and punished – lightly. But the final disgrace of the bastard had proved too much, and he had killed Pompilia and her so-called parents. His defence?

> I did
> God's bidding and man's duty. . . .
>   made legible once more
> Your own decree . . . all too faintly traced. . . .
> Absolve then me, law's mere executant!
> Protect your own defender, – save me, Sirs!

And save Rome too! For through the Court's brave decision now Utopia might follow:

> Rome rife with honest women and strong men,
> Manners reformed, old habits back once more,
> Customs that recognise the standard truth, –
> The wholesome household rule in force again,
> Husbands once more God's representative.

Plausible, but not entirely consistent and convincing, either in matter or manner: a superficial frankness and humility, sentimentality even, occasionally cracking and crumbling to reveal the underlying arrogance, cruelty and hate.

One would give much to have Violante's version of events, but she was lying dead in San Lorenzo church. Nor, apparently, was the relegated Canon Giuseppe Caponsacchi at the trial, though the Old Yellow Book contained the deposition that he made after his arrest while helping Pompilia to escape, and from this, and inevitably with memories of his own flight to Italy with Elizabeth, Browning created the dramatic monologue of Book 6. The young priest begins in no conciliatory manner by accusing his judges of negligence: 'I left Pompilia to your watch and ward,' and as a result 'the beauty of the world' – (another unconscious memory of Shakespeare) – 'the splendour of heaven' now lies dying. At length he begins to tell the story of his life: how he, of the noblest house in Arezzo, became a fribbling priest, until one night at the theatre the sight of Pompilia made him vow to take his vocation seriously. There follows the story of Guido's forged letters carried by his mistress-messenger; Pompilia's appeal, 'Take me to Rome!'; the flight on the festival of St George, the saint with whom Giuseppe identifies himself; their capture within sight of safety; their forcible and final separation. Yet, if he had failed to save Pompilia, Pompilia had saved him, and he adds a final insult to his judges:

> I assuredly did bow, was blessed
> By the revelation of Pompilia. There!
> Such is the final fact I fling you, Sirs,
> To mouth and mumble and misinterpret: there!

Finally, the stricken young priest implores them, in no very saintly fashion, not to condemn Guido to death, but to something worse: to slither down to Judas where each may tear the other in devil's fun to all eternity.

After St George's account of his failure to slay the dragon, Pompilia tells her story in Book 7, She begins like the innocent illiterate girl she is meant to be: 'I am just seventeen years and five months old,' describing quite simply, yet vividly, how she was sold to Guido when only a child, and his attempt with his go-between mistress to entangle her with Caponsacchi. She has Browning's gift of vivid description: old Guido,

> nothing like so tall as I myself
> Hook-nosed and yellow in a bush of beard,
> Much like a thing I saw on a boy's wrist,
> He called an owl and used for catching birds.

She even has, although unconsciously, Browning's satirical sense of humour, as when she recounts the Archbishop's reply to her appeal to put her in a convent:

> 'If motherhood be qualified impure,
> I catch you making God command Eve sin!'

And, like Browning himself, she knows what God thinks, and why He acts thus and thus: that, for example,

> a worm must turn
> If it would have its wrong observed by God.

In brief, Pompilia's monologue is by no means entirely dramatic, for Browning employs her as a mouthpiece for his teaching, his own religious opinions. These, for example, are scarcely the words of an illiterate girl:

> It may be idle or inopportune,
> But, true? – why, what was all I said but truth,
> Even when I found that such as are untrue
> Could only take the truth in through a lie?
> Now – I am speaking truth to the Truth's self:
> God will lend credit to my words this time.

Then Browning, most realistic, least sentimental, and in so many ways least Victorian of Victorian writers, oddly idealises, sentimentalises his heroine, dwelling on the pathos of the innocent's predicament, the motherless-father-less girl with a near-motherless-fatherless babe – 'No father . . . no, never had, I say!' – who forgives everybody, and even thanks Guido for saving her 'as by fire'. One thinks of the heroine, Mildred, in *A Blot in the 'Scutcheon*:

'I had no mother.' Yet pathos rises to tragedy in her last message to her soldier-saint:

> Do not the dead wear flowers when dressed for God?
> Say, – I am all in flowers from head to foot!

The poem reaches its climax with the dying words of Pompilia, and the two following Books are a relief from tension, much like the quiet Act IV of a Shakespearean tragedy, the lull that serves to heighten the ensuing catastrophe. Book 8, therefore, is the monologue of Hyacinthus de Archangelis, counsel for the defence, for Guido and (as an afterthought) his less gentlemanly associates: one of the most amusing satires that Browning ever wrote. The jovial gourmet, not in the least interested in Guido, but only in anticipating and defeating the arguments of the opposing counsel for Pompilia, is preparing the draft of his defence on his young son's birthday, which he so looks forward to celebrating later that thoughts of it are constantly breaking in. 'Honour' is the basis of his defence, for nothing can be excessive in avenging outraged honour, God's gift to man, and to prove his point he cites the bee and the elephant, quotes Solomon, Scaliger and Aelian, and asks,

> Shall man prove the insensible, the block,
> The blot o' the earth he crawls on to disgrace? . . .
> (May Gigia have remembered, nothing stings
> Fried liver out of its monotony
> Of richness, like a root of fennel, chopped
> Fine with the parsley . . .)

Then, after further quotation from the Classics and the Scriptures he is able to prove that the only way, the only legal way, in which to avenge outraged Honour is

> Back to its simple proper private way
> Of decent self-dealt gentlemanly death.

And he quotes the poor, dishonoured, distressed and weeping Guido himself:

> 'Restore the white was on that shield of mine
> Borne at' – wherever might be shield to bear.
> 'I see my grandsire, he who fought so well
> At' – here find out and put in time and place,
> Or else invent the fight his grandsire fought:
> 'I see this! I see that!'
> > (See nothing else,
> Or I shall scarce see lamb's fry in an hour!)

At last, 'Done i' the rough!' He can revise his script tomorrow, for now comes 'fry and family and friends. . . . Sing Tra-la-la,' and a final quotation, or mis-quotation, from Shakespeare: 'for lambkins, we must live!'

Bottinius's defence of Pompilia in Book 9 is not as outrageously funny as Archangeli's defence of Guido, though it is equally cynical, and contains a brilliant parenthetic and little-known anecdote meant to illustrate something or other. One night, Peter, John and Judas, tired and hungry, had to put up at an inn where the only food was a starveling fowl, enough only for one. So they agreed to sleep for an hour until it was cooked, and the one whose dream should prove the happiest was to have the prize. John dreamed that he was the Loved Disciple: 'Mine the meal!' Peter that he was given the keys of heaven: 'Mine the meal!' But Judas dreamed he dreamed:

> 'Methought I meanly chose to sleep no wink
> But wait until I heard my brethren snore;
> Then stole from couch, slipped noiseless o'er the planks,
> Slid downstairs, furtively approached the hearth,
> Found the fowl duly brown, both back and breast,
> Hissing in harmony with the cricket's chirp,
> Grilled to a point; said no grace but fell to,
> Nor finished till the skeleton lay bare.
> In penitence for which ignoble dream,
> Lo, I renounce my portion cheerfully!
> Fie on the flesh – be mine the ethereal gust,
> And yours the sublunary sustenance!
> See that whate'er be left ye give the poor!'
> Down the two scuttled, one on other's heel,
> Stung by a fell surmise; and found. . . .

Like any other Renaissance pedant, Bottinius cites the ancients at every opportunity, 'our one infallible guide', finishing with a reference to Isocrates and muttering as he lays down his pen:

> But all those ancients could say anything!
> He put in just what rushed into his head:
> While I shall have to prune and pare and print.
> This comes of being born in modern times
> With priests for auditory. Still, it pays.

After the fripperies of the opposing advocates, what may be called the last act of the tragedy begins with the Pope's soliloquy in Book 10 – begins, to Browning's delight, with unedifying anecdotes of former papal judgements. Then at last the old man, the octogenarian Innocent XII, turns to the case that he is called upon to judge, summarises the story, and comes to the same conclusion as Browning about the characters: Guido, the 'midmost blotch of black' in his horrible family; Pompilia, 'perfect in whiteness'; Violante-Pietro, 'sadly mixed natures'; Caponsacchi, 'the hero – pure – "Well done!" ' But what, the Pope asks, if he is wrong? he, God's representative on

> This one earth, out of all the multitude
> Of peopled worlds, as stars are now supposed, –
> Was chosen, and no sun-star of the swarm,
> For stage and scene of Thy transcendent act.

In the 17th century Popes did not believe in other earths, but forbade Galileo to say that this one moved, and this confusion of stars and planets is a disconcerting introduction to the philosophy that follows, Innocent's perhaps, but certainly Browning's. Man has strength and intelligence enough, he muses, but lacks a corresponding love, the base of the triangle:

> I reach into the dark,
> Feel what I cannot see, and still faith stands:
> I can believe this dread machinery
> Of sin and sorrow, would confound me else,
> Devised, – all pain, at most expenditure
> Of pain by Who devised pain, – to evolve,
> By new machinery in counterpart,
> The moral qualities of man – how else? –
> To make him love in turn and be beloved,
> Creative and self-sacrificing too,
> And thus eventually God-like. . . .
> Life is probation and the earth no goal
> But starting-point of man.

The old man grows garrulous, but conscientiously, if not very coherently, considers possible defences of Guido and pleas for mercy, until at length, with sudden decision:

> 'Who is upon the Lord's side?' asked the Count.
> I, who write –
> > On receipt of this command,
> Acquaint Count Guido and his fellows four
> They die to-morrow.'

The poem might have ended here, the Ring apparently complete, but fortunately Browning was even more interested in the ways of men and women than in the ways of God, more interested in Guido than in the Pope, and to Guido he devoted a second Book, the longest and best, the monologue

of Book 11. With just twelve hours to live, Guido speaks to his would-be
confessors, a Cardinal and an Abate whom he flatters and appeals to for help,
always protesting his innocence. In the good old days when men were men,
a noble could avenge an insult, kill an inferior with impunity and, indeed, be
congratulated, but this new-old Pope with his new-fangled interpretation of
the law has un-Romed Rome, and is himself the murderer. As time passes
he grows wilder, more hysterical, pleads for life, calls Cardinal and Abate
stupid, insolent, and tells them what he really meant do do: kill Violante,
Pietro and Pompilia, then swear that he found her in the embraces of the
cowardly Caponsacchi who escaped – but somehow she lived long enough to
tell another story. Cardinal, Abate, save me from 'that murderous old man!'
as good as dead. You, too, Abate, 'with that hacking cough', have not another
year to live; and as for you, Cardinal,

> Go eat your heart, you'll never be a Pope!
> Inform me, is it true you left your love,
> A Pucci, for promotion in the church?. . . .
>
> I use up my last strength to strike once more
> Old Pietro in the wine-house-gossip-face,
> To trample underfoot the whine and wile
> Of beast Violante, – and I grow one gorge
> To loathingly reject Pompilia's pale
> Poison my hunger took for food. . . .
> I lived and died a man, and take man's chance,
> Honest and bold: right will be done to such.
>
> Who are these you have let descend my stair? . . .
> Sirs, my first true word, all truth and no lie,
> Is – save me notwithstanding! Life is all! . . .
> Don't open! Hold me from them! . . .
> Abate, – Cardinal, – Christ, – Maria, – God, . . .
> Pompilia, will you let them murder me?

'*Murder* me'! For a comparable catastrophe we must go back to the Eliza-
bethans, to Marlowe and the last words of Faustus as the Devils approach
for their prey:

> O, mercy, heaven! look not so fierce on me!
> Adders and serpents, let me breathe a while!
> Ugly hell, gape not! come not, Lucifer!
> I'll burn my books! O Mephistopholis!

In Book 1 Browning had himself played Prologue to the Roman murder
story, and now in Book 12 he returned as Epilogue, to bring it to an end, 'had

anything an end.' Yet he introduced or re-introduced, four characters to help him perfect the Ring. First, a gay Venetian visitor to Rome who writes a Chaucerian, though heartless, letter to a friend, describing the execution of Guido and his four confederates in the Piazza del Popolo opposite the church of S. Maria,

> Where they possess, and showed in shrine today,
> The blessed *Umbilicus* of our Lord,
> (A relic 'tis believed no other church
> In Rome can boast of).

Then a letter from Guido's disappointed advocate Arcangeli, who took his little boy to see the fun, having promised him on his birthday that if he failed to save Count Guido's head he should at least 'go see it chopped from trunk.' To balance this there is a letter from Pompilia's advocate Bottini, now employed by the Convertite Convent to obtain the money she had bequeathed to her baby son. He defends his action by arguing that at the trial he was concerned with Guido's guilt, not with Pompilia's innocence, and angrily encloses the text of part of a sermon preached by a monk whose meddling had spoiled the freshness of the best points he had made. The sermon is Browning's, the text, 'God is true, and every man a liar,' meaning that man is too weak to perceive absolute truth, which he must learn to live and long for until one day, 'Approved by life's probation, he may speak.' Meanwhile, God does not always intervene to save the innocent, and many a pure Pompilia dies defeated by 'the world's calumny,/Stupidity, simplicity, – who cares?'

Browning was no Pangloss, believing that all is for the best in the best of all possible worlds, but he was an optimist in that he believed not only in God, but also in man, his ultimate triumph, and he believed that Art – painting, music, poetry – could help him towards the perception of truth. He ended his four-years' labour, therefore, with another address to his readers:

> So, British Public, who may like me yet,
> (Marry and amen!) learn one lesson hence
> Of many which whatever lives should teach:
> This lesson, that our human speech is naught,
> Our human testimony false, our fame
> And human estimation words and wind.
> Why take the artistic way to prove so much?
> Because, it is the glory and good of Art,
> That Art remains the one way possible
> Of speaking truth, to mouths like mine at least.

Even if the British Public did not yet like Browning, the critics were beginning to like him more and more. It is true that there were still complaints: some, apparently ignorant of prosody, were unable to scan his lines, others found the subject disagreeable; for a Catholic reviewer, the thoughts attributed to the Pope were highly improper, and, more delightfully, Caponsacchi was more like a young English parson than a Roman priest. But for others no praise could be too high: 'in the very first rank of English poets'; 'beyond all parallel the supremest poetical achievement of our time . . . the most precious and profound spiritual treasure that England has produced since the days of Shakespeare.' Even Swinburne was converted and called it a 'wonderful work', and more profoundly, for Buxton Forman this 'Epic of Psychology' was 'more essentially modern than any great poetic production of these latter centuries.'

He was right; with the publication of *The Ring and the Book* the modern movement in English poetry was fairly launched; the bardic tradition was threatened, and Hardy was to write how 'The bower we shrined to Tennyson is roof-wrecked.' The mythical hero, from Viking Beowulf to Victorian Arthur, was jostled by the psychologically more interesting real villain; and a greater realism of matter demanded a greater realism of manner, verse that was closer to ordinary speech than a conventional poetic diction. *The Ring and the Book* like *Paradise Lost* is written in blank verse, but verse that has more in common with Donne's, a subject that has more in common with the novels of Flaubert and Dostoevsky than with the epic of Milton.

More interesting than the opinions of his critics, however, is the opinion of Browning himself. Before Julia Wedgwood broke off her correspondence with him early in 1865 he had promised to show her his 'Poem' before it was published, and beginning on 5 November 1868 he sent her copies of the four volumes before they came out. She did not like them. Although she praised the 'stereoscopic view' – admirable phrase – there was too much black round the pure white of Pompilia. Browning admitted that perhaps he did 'unduly like the study of morbid cases of the soul,' but, given the subject, given the treatment, his business had been to explain *fact*, to change nothing, to add nothing. Yet out of all this evil good evolved, good to the priest, to Pompilia, to the Pope, and, 'I would fain hope, to who reads and applies my reasoning to his own experience.' Julia was unconvinced; she loved Pompilia and the Pope, but 'you present us with a wonderful variety of mud.' And Browning: 'It is a shame, that when there is anything you contrive to like in it, you cry out, "It's not yours, you know – only half yours," and so on: then comes an ugliness, and "Ah, there you are at home, – there I see you at work!" ' However, a fortnight later, on 12 February 1869, when he sent the last volume he wrote: 'My son is at Ch.Ch.: my owl is still on his perch: my book is out: my intention is to hear Joachim play to-night: my friend is my friend, all the more because of Guido and the Lawyers – "What can I want beside?" as the psalm asks.'

Their correspondence was almost over, but not quite. On Good Friday Julia confessed that the real reason for her asking him, four years ago, not to visit her again was not that their friendship was being misunderstood for something more, but that she had heard that he found it 'a gêne', a bother, a bore. Somewhat irritably he denied ever having said such a thing, though he finished his letter 'Yours affectionately now then and ever, R.B.' Yet it was the end of the affair.

13. Elizabeth and Pen in Rome, 1860. *Courtesy Balliol College, Oxford.*

14. Elizabeth's grave in Florence; she died 29 June 1861
Armstrong Browning Library.

15. The London to which Browning returned in 1861. Engraving by
Gustave Doré, *Mary Evans Picture Library.*

16. Browning in 1861.

17. Sarianna.

Courtesy Balliol College, Oxford.

18. 'Robert Browning takes tea with the Browning Society'—
caricature by Max Beerbohm. *Ashmolean Museum, Oxford.*

10. A Troubled Period
1869–77

'DEAREST Isa' remained however, even though in Florence. In January 1869, therefore, he wrote to tell her that Lady Stanley had summoned him by telegraph to go to a luncheon with 'Prince Christian and his kith and kin', though he did not add that a few weeks later he was to take tea with Queen Victoria. At about the same time he was offered the Lord Rectorship of St Andrew's University, the first of many similar invitations, all of which he declined, as he disliked making speeches. If the British Public did not yet like him, royalty and the best people did, a fact not unnoticed by little Alfred Austin, future Poet Laureate, who wrote of his 'looking for fame', and advised the 'general public to forswear Mr Browning and all his works', which were merely metrical prose.[13]

Austin's article did not appear until June, and in April Browning and Sarianne went to Paris for a month, but were back in time to visit Oxford and see Pen cox his college boat, which made five 'bumps' in the course of the week's races. His work was less satisfactory. 'Latin prose and Greek non satis,' Dean Liddell noted in June. He should have known, for he was the Liddell of the famous *Greek-English Lexicon* – and incidentally father of the girl for whom another Fellow of Christ Church, 'Lewis Carroll', had recently written *Alice in Wonderland*. He was now writing *Through the Looking-Glass*, and one cannot help wondering if he was having a sly dig at Browning in Alice's conversation with Humpty Dumpty, who could 'explain all the poems that ever were invented – and a good many that haven't been invented just yet,' from the hard words of 'Jabberwocky' to the inconclusions of 'I sent a message to the fish.'

Browning himself, had he known it, was about to enter a Wonderland, though one less amusing than Alice's. 'For the long vacation,' he wrote, 'I don't know what we shall do.' In fact the three of them went to Scotland with the Story family to stay with 'an old friend', or recent acquaintance, Lady Louisa Ashburton, at her house on Loch Luichart in the Highlands. A beautiful, talented and very wealthy widow of forty, she was apt to forget her social engagements, and was away when her guests arrived, so that they had to spend some time in whatever accommodation they could find. However, by the end of August their hostess had returned, and on the 28th Browning was able to tell Isa that 'all goes well now in this beautiful place.' Pen had got what he wanted – shooting and deer-stalking, and had just shot a splendid stag 'the head of which will glorify his rooms at Ch. Ch.'

What happened next is not very clear, but it was probably towards the middle of September that he made Lady Ashburton the offer of marriage about which he was to write to Story's daughter Edith some three years later: 'I suppose that Lady A. did not suppress what she considered the capital point of her quarrel with me when she foamed out into the couple of letters she bespattered me with, – yet the worst she charged me with was, – having said that my heart was buried in Florence, and the attractiveness of a marriage with her lay in its advantage to Pen – two simple facts.' It is almost incredible that the author of *Men and Women* and *The Ring and the Book* could have proposed to such a woman in such a way; yet we remember his father's unfortunate affair with another widow, and he was desperately worried about the idle Pen's future. Perhaps he was only being scrupulously honest in telling her about his devotion to his former wife and anxiety about her son, but no wonder he was indignantly repulsed, that a violent quarrel between two proud people followed, and that a defeated Browning suffered acute remorse for what he came to regard as his betrayal of Elizabeth – though her shade would forgive him, and, remembering his letter of 22 May 1845, merely smile at his customary clumsiness.

By the middle of September, now without Sarianna and Pen, he had moved south to Naworth Castle on the Border, where, worried 'pretty nearly to last degree', he was a guest of the Earl of Carlisle, who sketched him short-sightedly reading aloud from *The Ring and the Book*. After the Earl he was to stay with the Duchess of Cleveland, then Lady Alford, 'and after that, – whither, do you suppose?' Warwick Crescent, whence his letters to Isa reflect his disturbed state of mind, a new bitterness. We can understand why he should call Alfred Austin 'a filthy little snob' who noted how many dinners he ate in good company, but there is also a less generous note in his estimate of other poets. In his *Holy Grail* Tennyson described moonlight on a castle's towers instead of a conflict in a knight's soul; 'The monotony, however, you must expect – if the new is to be of a piece with the old.' Rossetti's just published *Poems*, recovered from his wife's grave where he had buried them –

surely Browning thought of Elizabeth? – were *'scented* with poetry. .... I hate the effeminacy of his school.' Swinburne's verses were 'florid impotence', the minimum of thought in the maximum of words. He admitted that he was little sympathetic to poetry of most sorts, and there was much truth in these criticisms, but they were uncharacteristic in their brutality. 'I am getting ill-natured,' he confessed, and perhaps it was at about this time that he wrote 'Gerousios Oinos' ('Wine of the Elders'), a short poem ridiculing the watered-down poetry of his contemporaries. In it he dreams that the great English poets of the past hold a feast, after which servingmen rush in to taste the remains, eking out what is left of the wine with water, beer and mundungus:

> Oh, England (I awoke and laughed)
> True wine thy lordly Poets quaffed,
> Yet left – for, what cared they! –
> Each glass its heel-tap – flavouring sup
> For flunkeys when, to liquor up,
> In swarmed – who, need I say!

Apparently Browning thought of including it in his *Jocoseria* of 1883, but it was no joke, or a very bad one, and fortunately he never published it.[14]

Meanwhile, in early 1870, his thoughts turned to Matthew Arnold's Gypsy-Scholar who gave a wistful look at 'The line of festal light in Christ-Church hall', and so, wistfully, back to Pen. By March, however, he was feeling better, for to his great delight his old friend Joseph Milsand was staying with him, his sense of humour returned, and he told Isa a most un-Victorian story that a lady had whispered to him at a dinner-party, and is worth recording as it tells us quite a lot about Browning:

A husband returns from the country, and begins to his wife 'Dear, to be frank, – I have failed in my duty to you: forgive me, – as I would forgive you, were it possible you could forget yourself so!' – She replies 'But since you put it so, – I forgive you – for I *do* need forgiveness likewise!' – 'Indeed! Well, – with whom was the fault we will agree to forget?' – 'With Mr —— the parson.' – 'And how many times did you err?' – 'Impossible to say – yet – there may be a method of knowing: he used to come to read the Holy Book to me, – and, whenever he began to be naughty, he, first of all, doubled down the page he left off at.' The Bible was produced, and found to be dogs' eared from Genesis to Revelation!
Come, now, dearest, have I helped your liver at all?

He barely mentioned Dickens, his exact contemporary, who died suddenly in June, and he had nothing to say about the momentous Education Act of the same month, but he had much to say about Pen's education. 'Most of my troubles happen in June,' he wrote. It was the month of Elizabeth's death, and now of her son's final Oxford failure in his examinations, and consequent removal from Christ Church. 'All I can do – except to give money – is *done* and done in vain,' he wrote bitterly to George Barrett; he was costing about £150 a term, a huge sum in those days. And to Isa: 'He wants the power of working, and I give it up in despair: but his natural abilities are considerable, – and he may turn out a success, after all, though not in the way which lay most naturally before him.' But why 'naturally'? Browning must have realised long before this time that the boy, the young man, was not a scholar, but an artist like his parents, interested in music and poetry, painting and sculpture, and he must have been partly to blame for Pen's failure, by forcing him to study Latin and Greek in which he was not interested, at the university from which he had himself in his youth been debarred.

Then, 'Here is the horrible war,' he wrote on 19 July, the day on which the Franco-Prussian War began, yet a month later, leaving Pen with a tutor, he and Sarianna went to St Aubin on the Normandy coast, where they were joined by Milsand. On 1 September came the French disaster at Sedan, followed by the abdication of Napoleon and fall of the Second Empire, and Browning and his sister at Milsand's insistence fled to England, with which normal communications had been severed, in a cattle-boat. 'The one sweet & comfortable fact is the advance on Rome,' Browning wrote on 19 September. On the following day, French troops having been withdrawn, Victor Emmanuel entered the real capital of Italy, while the Pope shut himself in the Vatican and excommunicated those who had deprived him of his former territory. 'How poor Florence will like the change is hardly a question,' Browning wrote, and he added more than a few words on Napoleon: 'he should be blotted out of the world as the greatest failure on record. . . . But there has been no knavery, only decline & fall of the faculties corporeal & mental . . . the wretched impostor . . . a lazy old and worn-out voluptuary. . . .'

He had much more to say about him in the poem that he had nearly finished, but meanwhile in the late spring of 1872 he wrote *Balaustion's Adventure*, what he called 'the most delightful of May-month amusements' in his dedication to the young and beautiful Countess Cowper, whose suggestion it was. But the real inspiration was Elizabeth, in honour of whom he prefaced his poem with a quotation from her 'Wine of Cyprus' celebrating 'Euripides, the human'. For *Balaustion* is an adaptation of the *Alcestis* of Euripides, last and most unconventional of the great Greek tragediens.

It begins with the adventure proper of Balaustion, a Rhodian girl who persuades others to sail with her to Athens when their island joins the Spartans in the Peloponnesian War. Driven by storm and pirates into hostile Syracuse, they are not allowed to land until the Syracusans discover that Balaustion is, like themselves, an admirer of Euripides. Enmity becomes amity and, standing on a temple steps, she half recites, half describes the *Alcestis*, 'That strangest, saddest, sweetest song', a performance of which she had recently seen: how King Admetus is promised immortality if his father, mother or wife will die instead of him, and his wife Alcestis gives her life, but is rescued from the clutch of Death by Herakles. 'What's poetry except a power that makes?' Balaustion asks, and herself answers, 'Who hears the poem, therefore, sees the play.' So does the reader, so vivid the description.

First we see the excitable young Balaustion who herself sees and describes the actors' faces behind their masks, an imaginative feat that rouses the wrath of 'a brisk little somebody,/Critic and whippersnapper' – so much for Alfred Austin. Then the wretched Admetus who quarrels with his father for refusing to die on his behalf, and the magnificent Herakles whose great voice and presence bring light, joy and love of man into the sombre scene: 'Come drink along with me,' – very different from Ben Ezra's 'Grow old along with me.' And Alcestis, the dear dead woman who, of course, for Browning was Elizabeth:

> the best of wives
> That ever was toward husband in this world! . . .
> A mere dead weight upon her husband's arm.

And it must have been with rueful thoughts of his late affair with Lady Ashburton that he wrote the dying words of Alcestis, who leaves her two children in her husband's care:

> 'Uphold them, make them masters of my house,
> Nor wed and give a step-dame to the pair. . . .
> The boy has got a father, a defence.'

And the sobbing Admetus:

> 'Fear not! And, since I had thee living, dead
> Alone wilt thou be called my wife. . . .
> And I shall bear for thee no year-long grief,
> But grief that lasts while my own days last, love! . . .
> For I shall end the feastings – social flow. . . .'

Then Balaustion describes how Herakles brings back Alcestis veiled, and tries to persuade Admetus to accept the unknown woman, but he refuses:

163

> Ah, but the tears come, find the words at fault!
> There is no telling how the hero twitched
> The veil off: and there stood, with such fixed eyes
> And such slow smile, Alkestis' silent self!
> It was the crowning grace of that great heart,
> To keep back joy: procrastinate the truth
> Until the wife, who had made proof and found
> The husband wanting, might essay once more,
> Hear, see, and feel him renovated now.

'Such fixed eyes and such slow smile.' It is Elizabeth – to the life.

Balaustion offers one criticism of the play: Admetus is unworthy of his wife. She would have made him a noble king for whom Alcestis secretly arranged with the gods that she should die so that he could continue his good work. But she adds another tribute to Euripides – another delightful anachronism, quoting Elizabeth:

> I know the poetess who graved in gold,
> Among her glories that shall never fade,
> This style and title for Euripides,
> *The Human with his droppings of warm tears.*

So the poem ends, as it began, with Elizabeth.

Despite the strictures of an obtuse *Times* reviewer, it soon went into a second edition – 'a good sale for the likes of me'. It deserved its popularity, for, though comparatively little-known today, it is one of the best of Browning's long poems, and the eager, imaginative Balaustion is unforgettable. Certainly her creator was not to forget her.

And Browning-Admetus was to keep his word with Alcestis-Elizabeth. He had resolved not to see Lady Ashburton again, but late in July he took Pen to Scotland to stay with his friend Ernest Benson near Pitlochry in the Highlands, where Pen spent his time shooting grouse while his father walked, read, played the piano and wrote. Jowett was close by with a reading-party, a member of which described how Browning was 'perpetrating "Hohenstiel Schwangau" at the rate of so many lines a day, neither more nor less.' He was enjoying himself in the quiet of a shooting-lodge some three miles from the house, having an impulse to write, and soon he would be quite on his own, as he told Isa, for Pen was to go to Lady Ashburton's to shoot deer. 'I shall not accompany him,' he added. Yet he did accompany him. There had been some sort of reconciliation with the Lady; he had sent her a copy of *Balaustion's Adventure,* and at length she persuaded him to visit her for a day. Early in October, therefore, he and Pen moved still farther north across the Highlands to Loch Luichart. There he saw her, but there was no renewal of marriage proposals, though some ado about letters, and it was not long before he was back in London.

Pen and Lady Ashburton. That all was not well with Browning after his return seems clear from his letters to Isa. Instead of being written on the 19th of the month they were now nearly always late, short, scrappy and concerned largely with his health: 'biliousness, and such a cold and cough. . . . I have been really unwell . . . bilious . . . this hateful climate . . . bilious and out of sorts.' However, in his letter of 'Oct. 19 – Nov 8!!' he told her that he was just about to take his new poem to his publisher, and in that of 'Dec 29 for 19' he assumed that she had received his 'little Book'. This was *Prince Hohenstiel-Schwangau: Saviour of Society*, a 2000-line monologue supposed to be spoken by Napoleon III shortly before Sedan and his flight to England where he was then living, or rather, dying. Browning had begun the poem in Rome in 1860 when angered by the Treaty of Villafranca which left Venetia in Austrian hands, but had written most of it in Scotland that autumn, by which time he had modified his opinion of the ex-Emperor, and characteristically gave him the chance to make the most of his good intentions. The reviewers, however, were baffled, one calling it 'a glorification', another 'a scandalous attack' on the old friend of England. It was neither, but why Browning himself should have thought it, as he told Isa, 'a sample of my very best work' passes understanding. Did he really think that the Prince's Apology was equal to those of Mr Sludge and Bishop Blougram? They are straightforward and amusing self-revelations, but *Hohenstiel* is neither straightforward nor amusing. It is true that there are perfectly lucid passages; the Prince is a conservator, he tells us, his object being to save society:

> To save society was well: the means
> Whereby to save it, – there begins the doubt –

and with the doubt begins the obscurity of dream within reality, of speech within speech, of sentences thirty lines or more long, until the reader loses himself in the labyrinth of parenthetic ambiguities, and his interest in the so elusive hero. The verse itself, turned out so many lines a day, has a soporific effect, so regular, so unvaried its iambic beat, so often abstract the vocabulary. It was a return to the obscurities without the poetry, of *Sordello*, and there was no Elizabeth to tell him so. But how she would have loved the half-dozen lines describing greybeards debating in a dimly-lighted council-chamber:

> and what they say is doubt,
> And what they think is fear, and what suspends
> The breath in them is not the plaster-patch
> Time disengages from the painted wall
> Where Rafael moulderingly bids adieu,
> Nor tick of the insect turning tapestry
> Which a queen's finger traced of old, to dust.

'In all my journeyings in Italy,' he wrote to Isa, 'I could never venture to leave the straight line of obligation. . . . Ba could not go, I could not leave her.' Thus, he had never seen, for example, such places as Etruscan Volterra and many-towered San Gimigniano. He was not complaining, nor did he add that his care for Elizabeth had restricted not only his travels but also his work. Now, however, he was free to write as he had written in the years before his marriage. Between 1833 and 1846 he had published three long poems, a play and the eight Numbers of 'Bells and Pomegranates', a book, or pamphlet, a year, from *Pauline* to *Luria*. In the twenty years 1847–67 he had added only three more volumes: *Christmas Eve and Easter Day*, *Men and Women* and *Dramatis Personae*. In the final twenty years of his life, however, he was to average again a volume a year, from the four volumes of *The Ring and the Book* in 1868–69 to *Asolando* in 1889. After the Italian interlude with Elizabeth, of occasional and inspired composition, there was a return to the wordy idiosyncrasies of his youth, though with a difference, an early, sometimes apologetic, over-exuberance being succeeded by the mature verbosity of a successful man contemptuous of his critics.

The Ring and the Book was, in a sense, his undoing. After writing a successful poem of more than 20,000 lines, to write one of a mere 2000 was little more than a month's entertainment, and as soon as he had finished *Prince Hohenstiel* he began another and longer poem, as he told Isa in December 1871: 'I am half way thro' another poem, of quite another kind.' Again, in the following January: 'I have just all but finished another poem of quite another kind.' And again, on 30 March: 'it is almost done: but I am very tired and bilious.' Perhaps, if he had not accepted an invitation to spend a week in the country with Lord Brownlow to meet his pretty Balaustion, Lady Cowper, he might have celebrated his 60th birthday with its publication on 7 May 1872, but it was to be the beginning of June before it appeared: *Fifine at the Fair*.

The scene is Pornic on an autumn afternoon, the day of the Fair on the Feast of St Gille, and in the lovely introductory lyric, 'Amphibian', Browning imagined himself swimming far out in the bay, all of the sea his own, when a sun-suffused butterfly appears, owning the sky instead. He, a living man, is also, in a sense, flying, though in a grosser element than that of the spirit of a dead woman, for so the butterfly appears to him, and he asks,

> Does she look, pity, wonder
> At one who mimics flight,
> Swims – heaven above, sea under
> Yet always earth in sight?

He had vowed never to begin a poem without thought of Elizabeth, and, indeed, the poem as a whole appears to have been inspired by her, or rather, like *Balaustion*, compelled by remorse verging on self-contempt for his near-desertion of her for Lady Ashburton whom he had so recently revisited. Written in the alexandrine couplets of Drayton's *Polyolbion* – the classical form of French verse, but in English a somewhat sing-song measure, the lines tending to fall into halves of three iambic feet – it is an episode in the life of a modern Don Juan, who walks through the Breton fair with his near-ethereal wife Elvire whom he finally deserts for the very womanly gipsy acrobat Fifine. The outline is simple enough, but the whole is a metaphysical confusion, half-waking half-dream, of the man's casuistical reasoning of how 'frenetic to be free', he can remain faithful to Elvire in the spirit while loving Fifine in the flesh, with dissertations on Helen, Cleopatra, Raphael, Schumann, painting, music, philosophy, religion, archaeology, in imagery derived from insects, fencing, stag-hunting and the sea – always the sea:

> I would there were one voyage, and then no more to do
> But tread the firmland, tempt the uncertain sea no more. . . .
> I would the steady voyage, and not the fitful trip, –
> Elvire, and not Fifine, – might test our seamanship.

But it is with Fifine, and not Elvire, that Don Juan embarks.

In the Epilogue, however, it is with Elizabeth that Browning is re-united as he sits wearily in his study:

> When, in a moment, just a knock, call, cry,
> Half a pang and all a rapture, there again were we! –
> 'What, and is it really you again?' quoth I:
> 'I again, what else did you expect?' quoth She.

Distractedly he begins to write a notice for insertion in a newspaper:

> '*Affliction sore long time he bore*, or, what is it to be?
> *Till God did please to grant him ease.* Do end!' quoth I:
> 'I end with – Love is all and Death is nought!' quoth She.

Again, unforgettable. And the best of *Fifine* is its Prologue and Epilogue. Though the beginning and end of the poem, the story proper, are absorbingly dramatic, the philosophic middle is distended out of all proportion. It is true that there are fine and deeply interesting passages, and the reader can concentrate for a time on a few of the century or so of sections into which it is divided, but after that the mind wearies. It is too long, too complex, to hold the attention, to be read for the pleasure of poetry.

Fifine led to one unhappy incident. Among the poems that Rossetti published in 1870 was 'Jenny', a dramatic monologue in the manner of Browning whose work he so much admired; the theme not unlike that of *Fifine*, the meditation of another Don Juan about a prostitute. It was attacked by Robert Buchanan in his article 'The Fleshly School of Poetry', and when Rossetti read *Fifine*, for some reason or other he thought that Browning, who had sent him a copy, had joined Buchanan in his attack, and the long friendship, which had begun in the early days of the Pre-Raphaelites, was at an end.

However, another friendship had been renewed. '*Waring* came home the other day,' Browning wrote to Isa in March. Alfred Domett, who had given them all the slip thirty years before, had just returned from New Zealand, of which for a short time he had been Prime Minister. Their correspondence had lapsed since the death of Elizabeth, but he lost no time in calling at Warwick Crescent, as he recorded in the Diary that he now began to keep.[15] Browning was out, but Sarianna, little changed by the years, welcomed him warmly in her 'old frank and slightly energetic style', and introduced him to Pen, who seemed an 'amiable young fellow'. As Browning was engaged every evening for the next week, they invited him to lunch, at which he met Milsand, but had nothing to say about Browning, except that he had not lost the good-humoured patience with which he would listen to friendly criticism of his work. Domett himself wanted friendly criticism of his own work, for he had returned with a long poem about New Zealand, *Ranolf and Amohia*; and Browning gave it: 'a great and astonishing performance.' He also tried to find him a publisher, but failed, and later in the year Domett published it, not unsuccessfully, at his own expense.

Meanwhile, leaving Pen to shoot grouse and deer in Scotland, Browning had taken Sarianna again to St Aubin, where Milsand was staying, and nearby was Anne Thackeray, the novelist's daughter, who christened the sleepy Normandy countryside 'White Cotton Night-Cap Country' because of the women's white head-dresses. In September they moved to Fontainebleau, to see Milsand back on his way to Dijon for the grape-harvest, and from there on the 19th – 'Not that it is really the 19th' – Browning wrote to Isa: 'I bring back with me, for winter-work in London, a capital brand-new subject for my next poem.' It was Milsand who had given him the subject, told him the melodramatic St Aubin story, and he had spent his Normandy holiday collecting material. Back in London, he began his winter-work on 1 December, and finished on 23 January 1873 – three days after Isa Blagden's death in Florence, where, like Elizabeth, she was buried. Browning was asked to subscribe towards an edition of her poems, but refused. The editor was to be Alfred Austin, and he wrote: 'When the book is perpetrated, – I may buy it, and, by help of penknife and ink-blotting, purify and render it fit to be read – for so I understand the "mark of friendship" you expect of me.'

Publication of *Red Cotton Night-Cap Country, or Turf and Towers* was delayed until May, for as the events described were very recent, to avoid a possible libel action, Browning was advised to make alterations, particularly of names. He had changed Anne Thackeray's 'White Cotton' to 'Red' to symbolise the blood of his melodrama – as well as the flag of the short-lived Paris Commune of 1871 – and at the beginning of the poem he imagines himself showing her the scene where the events took place.

Monsieur Léonce Miranda (really Antoine Mellerio), a generous, wealthy, profligate young man, carries off another man's wife to be his mistress in his Normandy country house, which he rebuilds with a belvedere, or tower. His mother summons him to Paris to reprove him for his extravagance, and in remorse he tries to drown himself in the Seine. Soon afterwards she dies, and this time he plunges both hands into a fire and burns them to the bone. Finally, he jumps from his tower down to the turf below and kills himself. He leaves his estate to his mistress, after whose death it is to go to the Church, a will that is upheld by the Court when disputed by his cousins.

Such was the story, and Browning followed it faithfully, but, as always, he was interested not so much in the action as in the thought that determines speech, the motive that prompts action. And here, as prologue to Miranda's 300-line soliloquy before his fatal leap – described in four lines – he explains, more fully perhaps than elsewhere, his dramatic creed and method:

> He thought – (Suppose I should prefer 'He said?'
> Along with every act – and speech is act –
> There go, a multitude impalpable
> To ordinary human faculty,
> The thoughts which give the act significance.

Who is a poet needs must apprehend
Alike both speech and thoughts which prompt to speak.
Part these, and thought withdraws to poetry:
Speech is reported in the newspaper.)

So, according to Browning, Léonce thinks: he has lacked faith, but now to prove his faith, faith that angels will carry him safely to the distant shrine, so that thousands will see his flight and testify that the age of miracles and faith is not over. So, a leap, a flash, and dead he lies on the turf. 'Mad!' 'No! sane,' says Browning:

Hold a belief, you only half-believe. . . .
Put faith to proof, be cured or killed at once!

Domett thought it a pity that Browning had written so rapidly – more than 4000 lines in less than 8 weeks – and he misquoted Byron: 'Your easy writing is sometimes d——d hard reading,' a dictum that his detractors might use against him. A few critics did complain of obscurity, but others found no lack of clarity; the poem, if it could be called a poem, was all too clear, a 'horrible and revolting' story, 'its essential spirit of immorality'. This, of course, is Victorian humbug; the poem is a graphic presentation of real, though admittedly abnormal, life, with an almost Shakespearean interpretation of motive, and its real failing is its length. If only the elderly Browning, like the poet of the middle, Elizabethan-Italian years, had controlled his excited imagination, had resisted the temptation to expand, inflate, digress, if *Red Cotton Night-Cap Country* had been reduced to half its length, it would not today be almost forgotten and very rarely read. And yet it was one of his most influential, forward-looking poems. 'Nobody out of Bedlam ever before thought of choosing such a theme,' Carlyle remarked. He would scarcely have said that a century later.

Browning sent a copy to Domett, who noted in his Diary that his photograph was 'in most of the shop windows', the one he liked best, the smiling one of his full face, which gave the best idea of 'his broad massive head and wide-spreading brows and full though not very open eyes.' He had introduced Domett to an old friend, Frederick Leighton's sister, Mrs Sutherland Orr, an intelligent widow who had recently settled in London, and was collecting material for her 'Life of Browning', published shortly after his death. In it she had much to say about another old friend of Browning's, Miss Egerton Smith, whom he had met when she visited Florence. Although very wealthy, she led a secluded life in London, unlike Browning, but like him had a passion for music, would call for him in her carriage, and together they would go to as many concerts as they could. And it was she who suggested in the summer of 1874 that they and Sarianna should have a holiday together at Mers, a hamlet near Tréport on the Normandy coast. It was there that Browning wrote the greater part of *Aristophanes' Apology*. He had already made a translation of Euripides' *Hercules Furens*, or 'Herakles' as he called it, and this he now incorporated in his new poem about the heroine of *Balaustion's Adventure*: how, after the death of Euripides, Balaustion argues with the half-drunk Aristophanes about the relative merits of tragedy and comedy, she maintaining that tragedy is the profounder more inspiring art, and to support her claim she reads the *Herakles*.

The poem of nearly 6000 lines was published in April 1875 as '*Aristophanes' Apology*; Including a Transcript from Euripides; Being the Last Adventure of Balaustion.' Critics were divided: it was a return to the 'confused wordiness ' of *Sordello*; 'not a sentence is superfluous'. Browning was particularly irritated by one review suggesting that the Honorary Fellow of Balliol was indebted to its Master, Jowett. Oddly enough, Carlyle liked it, told Browning that translating Greek tragedy was his real vocation, but asked why he could not have written in a plain straightforward manner. 'As if,' Browning said to Domett, 'this did not just make all the difference between a poet's treatment of a subject and a historian's.' But Domett protested that he expected too much of his readers, that as only a few scholars would understand all his classical allusions he had wilfully restricted their number; and Browning admitted that he was not likely to try anything of the same sort again. Domett was right; few have read, and few will read *Aristophanes' Apology*. It is too long, too difficult, and lacks the inspiration of *Balaustion's Adventure*. After writing tens of thousands of lines of blank verse, Browning could turn it out as easily as prose, and he was not a great prose writer. Of course there are memorable lines: 'All thy white wonder fainting out in ash,' for example, and,

> How the sea helps! How rose-smit earth will rise
> Breast-high thence, some bright morning, and be Rhodes!

But the best passage in the poem is the *terza rima* of Aristophanes' concluding song:

> Thamuris, marching, laughed 'Each flake of foam'
> (As sparklingly the ripple raced him by)
> 'Mocks slower clouds adrift in the blue dome!'
>
> For Autumn was the season; red the sky
> Held morn's conclusive signet of the sun
> To break the mists up, bid them blaze and die. . . .

If Browning was disappointed by the reception of his poem, he was more than delighted by the progress of Pen who, instead of shooting wild life, had begun to paint still life. He was studying in Antwerp, and Browning proudly showed Domett a Browningesque grotesquerie of a skeleton in a black cloak, and another of 'an old man contemplating the old skull'. A few months later he told him that Pen had had a wonderful success; the artist Rudolf Lehmann had bought one of his pictures for 150 guineas, and a lady had commissioned a portrait of herself for 40 guineas. Browning, Domett noted, 'was thoroughly hearty and genial – even more than usual on this occasion.'

That occasion was in March 1876, but meanwhile, in June-July 1875, Browning had written another poem, the 3000 lines of *The Inn Album*. Then, with Sarianna and Anne Egerton Smith, he had taken proofs to Villers-sur-Mer in Normandy for correction before publication in November. The plot was founded on fact, and he told Domett that he had intended to make a play of it – one thinks of *A Blot in the 'Scutcheon* – but, as Tennyson was writing the tragedy of *Queen Mary*, had decided on a hybrid form, half play half dramatic poem: the story of a young man's killing an elderly roué who had seduced the woman he loved. Ironically, the action is confined to a bright May morning, and there are only four characters, but as they are nameless another difficulty is added to the reading. Yet, in spite of the critics of the day, Henry James among them, there is little obscurity, and the main objection was to the story: 'coarse', 'vulgar', 'repulsive'. Young Robert Louis Stevenson – he was only 25 – had something to say about the style:

> When he finds a line shambling out from underneath him in a loose mass of unaccented syllables; when he finds it, like an ill-made blancmange, subside into a squash or quagmire instead of standing on its own basis with a certain sort of dignity or strength – quick, says Mr B., break it up into an unexpected parenthesis, choke off the reader with a dash, leave him clinging at the verse's end to a projecting conjunction, cut a somersault before him, flick off his hat. . . . in short, do what you will so you bewilder him, and the limping verse will get away to cover undetected.

It is entertaining nonsense with a grain of truth, but Stevenson might have quoted the apology that the author put into the villain's mouth:

> That bard's a Browning; he neglects the form:
> But ah, the sense, ye gods, the weighty sense!

The real defect of the poem, however, is its length: an admirable beginning and a splendidly dramatic, or melodramatic, ending, but again a grossly in-flated middle of speeches a hundred lines long.

Not long after its publication another volume was in the press, and in July 1876 it appeared as *Pacchiarotto and How He Worked in Distemper: With Other Poems*. Most of them had been written earlier in the year and were a welcome return to the shorter poems published before *The Ring and the Book*, though with a difference: instead of being 'dramatic', the speech of imaginary characters, Browning himself is nearly always, and sometimes the satirical, speaker. Thus in 'Pacchiarotto', named after an obscure 16th-century Sienese painter, he turned at last, in deliberately uncouth hudibrastic rhyme, on the critics who had baited him for the last forty years:

> An old friend – put leg forward nimbly
> 'We critics as sweeps out your chimbly!
> Much soot to remove from your flue, Sir! . . .

And more particularly did he discharge ill-temperedly the slops from his basin on the unfortunate Alfred Austin:

> While as for Quilp-Hop-o'-my-Thumb there,
> Banjo-Byron that twangs the strum-strum there –
> He'll think, as the pickle he curses,
> I've discharged on his pate his own verses!

'Philippo Baldinucci' is another satire, an amusing story of how the 17th-century Jews of Florence outwitted their Christian persecutors. Even better, and one of Browning's own favourite poems, written in his earlier manner, is 'A Forgiveness', a grandee's confession of why and how he killed his unfaithful wife, a story with an unforgettable description of the fatal weapon – 'Horror coquetting with voluptuousness' – and a characteristically startling conclusion. But best of all is 'St Martin's Summer', ostensibly dramatic, but really a profoundly personal poem about the ghost of Elizabeth and the 'breathing Beauty', Lady Ashburton, a return to the remorse of *Balaustion*:

> Where we plan our dwelling
>   Glooms a graveyard surely!
>   Headstone, footstone moss may drape, –
> Name, date, violets hide from spelling, –
>   But, though corpses rot obscurely,
>   Ghosts escape. . . .
> Ay, dead loves are the potent!
>   Like any cloud they used you,
>   Mere semblance you, but substance they!
> Build we no mansion, weave we no tent!
>   Mere flesh – their spirit interfused you!
>   Hence, I say!

For 'they' 'their' read 'she' 'her' and the meaning becomes apparent. The Prologue, too, is addressed to Elizabeth, and the Epilogue begins with a quotation from 'the dearest poet I ever knew', from her 'Wine of Cyprus', and wine is the image Browning develops to describe his own poetry: too rough, too strong, for his contemporaries but, after maturing, for tasters at the century's end it will be both strong and sweet:

> Mighty and mellow are never mixed,
> Though mighty and mellow be born at once.
> Sweet for the future, – strong for the nonce!

He was right. One critic assured him that 'in *Pacchiarotto* there is as little wisdom as poetry,' and Edward Dowden found it only an average vintage. But there can be few readers today who do not find both strength and sweetness in at least half of the poems in this volume of 1876.

Domett had little to say about Browning in 1876, and nothing about *Pacchiarotto*, but early in the following year – that of Queen Victoria's assumption of the title of Empress of India – he had a long chat with him and Sarianna, Pen still being in Antwerp painting. Among other things, Browning said he had a good mind to translate another Greek play to please Carlyle who liked his versions of the *Alcestis* and *Hercules Furens*, and when Domett returned from a tour of the West County in October he found a copy of the *Agamemnon* of Aeschylus waiting for him. It was dedicated to Browning's 'venerated friend Thomas Carlyle'. But Carlyle protested that he could not understand it: 'O dear! he's a very foolish fellow. He picks you out the English for the Greek word by word' – which was approximately what Browning had set out to do, and he was particularly annoyed by one reviewer who accused him of trampling 'upon his mother tongue with the hoofs of a buffalo'. Such a work, however, was not for the ordinary reviewer but for the classical scholar, and one of them at least was full of praise for the fearless audacity of the poet who employed 'that vast structural power over language, which he alone of men possesses.' Yet Browning's version *is* difficult, largely because it is a literal rendering of a corrupt and mutilated text, and it may be that Browning, a forward-marcher like his favourite Euripides, was protesting, as Mrs Orr maintained, against what he considered the extravagant claims that the Victorians made for the father of Greek tragedy, Aeschylus.

While Domett had been exploring Cornwall, Browning and Sarianna had joined Anne Egerton Smith at a villa she had taken, 'La Saisiaz', a few miles south of Geneva, and when at the beginning of December Dormett called to